LOSING
EVERYTHING

A MEMOIR

DAVID LOZELL MARTIN

Simon & Schuster
New York London Toronto Sydney

To Samuel

Simon & Schuster
1230 Avenue of the Americas
New York, NY 10020

First Simon & Schuster hardcover edition January 2009

SIMON & SCHUSTER and colophon are registered trademarks of Simon & Schuster, Inc.

For information about special discounts for bulk purchases,
please contact Simon & Schuster Special Sales at 1-800-456-6798
or business@simonandschuster.com.

Designed by Ruth Lee-Mui

Manufactured in the United States of America

1   3   5   7   9   10   8   6   4   2

Library of Congress Cataloging-in-Publication Data

Martin, David Lozell.
Losing everything / David Lozell Martin.
p. cm.
1. Martin, David Lozell.   2. Authors, American—20th
century—Biography.   I. Title.
PS3563.A72329Z46 2008
813'.54—dc22
[B]   2008036521

ISBN-13: 978-0-7432-9434-8

THE MORE LOST I GET,
THE CLOSER TO HOME I COME

I OWNED A farm in West Virginia with my wife and we lived there twelve years, the best years of my life. It was an old farm, settled a hundred years ago, a house built from timber cut on the property. Most of the land went up and down and rarely ran flat. No one had lived on the place full time for at least a decade before we got there. We brought the farm back to life as time and money allowed. We raised horses and cattle along with . . . ducks, cats, dogs, chickens, geese, and a parrot. Also, a brother, friends in crises, sons, friends of sons, a daughter of friends—who came to stay with us at various times for various lengths of times. I earned a living, sometimes thinly and other times fat, as a novelist. Often you hear people say they didn't know how good they had something until they lost it, but my wife and I knew we had a good life. We even admitted to the same dark dread, that one day someone from the Department of Responsible Adulthood would drive up our lane to tell us we had to stop playing around out in the country and go back to the city to get jobs like Responsible Adults.

Living on our farm those twelve years, we met artists and horse trainers, sculptors and poets, and at least one philosopher, Bob Neff. I think of him as Wisdom on the Mountain and would occasionally make my trek to Bob, like a *New Yorker* cartoon showing a pilgrim climbing to a mountaintop guru, to ask what he thought about something. Bob didn't always have answers, but he always had thoughts.

We also made friends with a retired building contractor who was a gunsmith and a composer of classical music. One midsummer evening we were planning a dinner out with this friend, Ed Lockwood, and his wife, Judy. Ed is from New Jersey, a dese and doze kind of guy, outrageously conservative by my way of thinking, anti-intellectual, and yet a brilliant natural pianist and self-taught composer who, at the collapse of the Soviet Union, composed and played a musical piece called "The Death of Russia" that brought tears to my eyes. Such was the magic of those years on our West Virginia farm we called Blue Goose.

Before Ed and Judy arrived, a thunderstorm had hit, short but violent. After the storm ended, my wife wanted to call the horses down to make sure they were safe because during the storm six of them had run from their pasture into the forest, which of course was the worst place to be during high wind and hellacious lightning. Five of the six came at her call, and I said I would walk up into the woods to see if I could find the sixth, Annie. I was wearing khakis and a checked shirt, cowboy boots, hardly the outfit for a trek through the trees, but I thought I would quickly find Annie cowering somewhere and get behind her and clap my hands and she'd run for home. I didn't bring a rope or bridle, not even a walking stick, much less a flashlight. It was a summer's evening and night was a hundred miles away. Just as I was heading into the woods, I looked back toward our house and saw Ed and Judy drive up. My wife would explain what was happening and I'd return in a few minutes and our evening could proceed as planned.

Living on a farm and spending time outside connects you with the weather and the smells and sounds of nature in ways denied us when we live in the city and work behind sealed windows under fluorescent lights, as I now do. Back on Blue Goose, it had been muggy before the storm, but afterwards, as I entered the forest and began climbing the first hill, the air was clean and cool.

All of our woods were on slopes; everything flat had long ago been cleared for fields and pastures. So I climbed ever upward, bushes and leaves soaking wet from the thunderstorm. I'd have to change clothes when I got back home—which would delay our dinner and then I'd hear about that from Ed all evening long. I was probably smiling in anticipation of some of the outrageous things he would say . . . when I saw Annie's trail.

You didn't have to be a tracker to see where she'd gone, her hooves had torn up the ground and she had broken branches along the way. She must've been hauling ass. Horses don't like to be separated from their herds, so I figured over the next ridge I'd see her standing there wondering where she was and how the blazes was she going to get back home—and if I didn't see her on the next ridge, then surely the one after that. I came to the fence marking our property. The storm had toppled a huge red oak tree, flattening a section of the fence, and I could see where Annie had picked her way through the limbs of the downed tree and off our property. I guess the lightning had terrified her. Most of what you can understand about horses comes from knowing they are prey animals.

As I followed her trail, I speculated she'd been standing under the tree when the storm hit and maybe she'd been injured by lightning or falling limbs. The previous year we'd found a neighbor's horse in the woods, struck by lightning, all four hooves exploded, the carcass feasted on by a flight of buzzards.

I stopped for a decision. I could go back now, change clothes, and we could still make it to a late dinner. But I doubted my wife would go to dinner if Annie was still unaccounted for, roaming on someone else's property, perhaps injured. So we *wouldn't* go to dinner if I came home without the horse. Okay, I'd follow Annie's trail and bring her home and if that made the hour too late to go to a restaurant, then we could have dinner at our house instead.

I continued following the trail. In a thick, hilly forest in the middle of summer when all the leaves are out, you rarely get a perspective beyond twenty yards or so. I couldn't tell if Annie was just ahead or nowhere near. All I could see was a few yards of the leafy trail in front of me, and all I had to follow was the path a frightened horse had left—still distinctly marked.

As I walked and climbed and walked, the forest changed. The area I was in now had been cut over and was so spare in places that I lost the horse's trail and had to range back and forth to pick it up again. Up until that point, following Annie had been easy—now it was a challenge, the forest floor rocky with thin soil and only a scattering of leaf debris for hooves to mark. Now I could see farther ahead—but still no horse in sight.

I walked on for an hour more, then another hour, screw dinner, I was bringing this damn horse home one way or the other. I felt savvy each time I found a mark on the ground, a twig recently broken—I was David, scout.

Then there she was, a big nervous bay filly. She had no halter. Because our horses had access to forest, we didn't always put halters on them when they were out to pasture for fear that they would scratch on a tree limb and get their halter hung up. The top straps on the halters we did use, called breakaway halters, were made of leather, which a struggling horse can break to free itself—unlike what'll happen with an all-nylon halter, which can get hung up and hold a horse until it breaks its neck trying to get loose. Horses are an exotic combination of speed and fragility, flightiness and stamina, always ready to run, always convinced something is giving chase. They can fall through a bridge and stand up, shake themselves off, and go on as if nothing happened—or they can gently slip on slick concrete and break a leg, split a hip, never get up.

This particular halter-less horse, Annie, was lost and close to panic when she saw me coming through the woods. I reached her and put a hand to her neck and she actually leaned against me as if to say, Thank God you're here—let's go home. I took off my dress belt and put it around her neck, not that it would restrain her if she wanted to run but it gave me something to hold as we would have to return along the same steep, slick terrain we had just covered.

First, I checked her for injuries, running a hand along her neck

4

and sides, down her legs, pulling on her fetlocks to make her raise her hooves so I could see if they were all right. She was fine, just scared and lost. Okay, time to go. I grabbed the belt and turned my horse for home.

What I saw made me gasp. Night was standing there. Just behind me. It had been following. I apparently had been traveling west toward a sky made lighter by the setting sun because when I turned around, away from that lighter sky, the woods were dark. Night out of the east had been trailing me as I had been trailing Annie.

I stood a minute or so, blinking, wondering what the hell was I going to do. By the time I looked again in the other direction, presumably west, the sun was gone and night had taken the occasion to throw itself completely around me and my horse.

I wasn't wearing a watch but estimated I had been gone for a few hours and wondered how deeply into a forest a man and a horse can get walking for a few hours.

We lived in an isolated part of West Virginia, with farms and settlements along valleys and rivers but few people living in the hundreds of miles of mountainous forests between those valleys and rivers. Farms in our area faced the creeks and valleys, turning their backs on the mountains. Nothing was up there . . . up *here* where Annie and I were. Nothing civilized.

My wife would occasionally go riding on old logging trails through these mountains and sometimes she'd come upon people unlike anyone we'd ever met—not just country folks but strange people who, we were later told, collected forest products, moss for florists and salamanders for fishermen, and lived not only off the electrical grid but off the grid of civilization. Their children didn't go to school. Their families were on no government roll. They weren't taxed or counted. I used these folks or rumors about them as a basis for characters in one of my novels. I called them the *barely people*—because in the book, they were people . . . but barely.

So now I'm leading Annie with my belt around her neck, it's dark and I'm wondering who else might be in this forest through which I'm trespassing, and what's going to happen if Annie and I fall off a ridge in this darkness and break a human or horse leg? Still, I couldn't just stand where I was until morning. Annie and I moved out cautiously.

I had lost all bearings for finding the trails we had made, for finding the way back to my property, but I came upon a game trail that we could follow even in the dark. As the night dipped deeper and moved in closer, I stopped telling Annie this was all her fault and told her instead that we are in this together so that if some barely person, coyote, wolf, panther, bear steps into this game trail a few yards ahead of us, I don't want you pulling loose and running your scared horse's ass off into the woods to leave me here all alone, I expect you to stick with me so we can face the danger together.

As they say, if horses could laugh . . .

Eventually I stopped walking. This is ridiculous, I decided. The hour must be closing in on midnight by now. I know the neighbors who live along the road, Big Branch, where our farm is located but I don't know anyone who lives *behind* us, in the mountains, in the woods, in the uncharted wilderness where I and Annie were now lost—so where was I going? My wife and friends would be worried. Search parties would be organized. But no one's going to be foolish enough to launch a search in these mountains in the middle of the night. The weather was warm, they would let me spend the night in the woods and then come looking for me at dawn. I tried shouting a few times and then listening hard for a reply . . . like shouting in outer space.

An old piece of woodsman advice is to follow a waterway downstream because eventually that creek will join another creek that will find a river—and along a river, people live. But Annie and I had been at the bottom of several ravines that were dry. Apparently, woodsman's advice is predicated on *finding* a waterway. Annie and I had found nothing but mountains and trees. So. The thing to do, I thought, Annie and I will stay here in these woods until morning and not keep wandering around to risk breaking our legs falling off a mountain in the dark.

I wasn't going to be able to hold on to the belt all night long, however, and if I let go I figured she'd wander off and then regardless of when I was rescued in the morning, we'd all have to go out again to find the damn horse. If I had a rope, I could tie her to a tree. If I had bacon and eggs, I could have supper . . . if I had a frying pan and a fire.

I was standing there trying to figure out how to secure Annie for the night when I heard a cow. This was good news. People don't turn their cattle loose into the mountains. A cow meant a pasture, which meant a farm.

I re-gripped the belt and led Annie toward the sound of the cow. She smelled them as we approached. I don't know if she thought these were our cows and she was home or if she was scared or what, but she became antsy and prancy and I was having the devil's own time controlling her with nothing but a dress belt looped around her neck.

Before, when we were lost in the deep forest, she had been a model of decorum, walking carefully and bumping against me for reassurance. But now she was nervous, snorting.

We found cows wandering through some open areas along a creek. With the tree canopy broken, the night sky offered light enough we could see to follow first the creek and then the cow trails away from the creek.

My best hope was to come to a pasture next to a road, find a gate and get on that road, and hope someone comes by who will tell me where I am. I'll ask that person to call my wife.

My worst fear, soon realized, was coming to a farmhouse. It would be bad enough, dangerous enough, to find yourself at midnight coming to an isolated farmhouse from the road, from the front—but walking up to that house in the middle of the night *from the back*, from the mountains and woods, that's trespassing and it can get someone, like me, shot. During the day, it's not unknown for strangers to come to a farmhouse from the road—delivering a package, lost and asking for directions, even trying to sell something. But, day or night, no one comes from behind you, walking out from your own property, already trespassing. How'd they get back there and why are they sneaking up on you? The fact it was past midnight made matters all the worse, which I believe is one of life's truths, that matters become worse after midnight.

So there's this farmhouse. No lights on, of course, not at this hour. And I'm standing there with a horse, we're well behind the house, back in the barnyard. Thank God I had the horse, at least she gave me an excuse—I got lost looking for my horse, I could tell the suspicious farmer, see . . . this horse right here.

I stood a long while trying to figure out what to do, how to do it. Could I just walk right past the house and down the lane and out to whatever main road the lane connected to? What if the farmer heard us and looked out his window and saw someone in his yard in the middle of the night? It's not like living in the city where people might be walking by your house at odd hours. Being in a farmer's yard, un-invited, after midnight was the equivalent of being in a city dweller's living room—with one serious difference. If you live in the city and see someone in your living room, you call 911. If you're on a farm and see someone in your yard after midnight, you call on Mr. Colt. I could be shot from a window and then, during the investigation of the shooting, when it came out that I was just a poor lost slob leading a lost horse, people would say what a shame, such an unfortunate mis-take, but no one would blame the farmer for shooting me.

My more immediate concern, however, was dogs. Every farm has dogs. They're usually turned loose at night to run off intruders, four-legged and two-legged. As soon as this farm's dogs get a whiff of me and Annie, there's going to be a storm of barking, the farmer will wake up and grab his nearest firearm, Annie will run off leaving me with no excuse for being there, and I'm going to get bitten or shot or both.

I'm scared of dogs I don't know. I've had dogs all my life and I've written about them in all of my books; I love dogs. But twice when I was growing up in the country I was attacked by dogs I didn't know, and those attacks left me with a lifelong fear. Once I know a dog, have been introduced to it, then I'm okay, it doesn't matter if it's a rottwei-ler or pit bull.

But I didn't know this farm and I didn't know its dogs and I was scared. I gripped the belt around Annie's neck and briefly considered hoisting myself aboard to ride through the yard bareback, hell-bent and not stopping for dogs with teeth or farmers with guns. But my wife was the equestrian in the family, not me. Without stirrups or reins or a saddle with a horn to hold tightly to, I could see myself getting thrown off and landing in the middle of the pack of snarling killer dogs, as per my midnight imagination.

I considered turning around and walking back into the woods and spending the night, then I could come up to the house in the morning when the farmer might be out and able to hold off his hounds. I just continued standing there, immobile with doubt and fear, appreciating what the phrase "screwing up your courage" really meant, and when I finally got it screwed as tightly as it was going to go, I tugged on Annie and walked toward the house, deciding to announce myself rather than trying to sneak past.

"Hello in the house!" My voice sounded weak. *"Hello in the house!"*

I braced for dogs.

Hollered again.

Waited for a light to come on.

Nothing. No dogs, no lights.

This was amazing, unexpected, eerie. I lead Annie as quickly as I could past the farmhouse, out a short lane, and onto a country highway. Happy! Now I didn't care what happened. I was out on a public thoroughfare. I had survived the ghost house without dogs or inhabitants. God knows where I was, one of those haunted areas of West Virginia where farmers long dead still rise at dawn to milk their ghostly cows. A variety of horror stories arrived uninvited in my mind as I waited for someone to drive by on this deserted hardtop road at whatever ungodly hour it had become.

Annie was skittish out on the road so I walked her along the shoulder, which is when I realized a river passed nearby. My God, how lost was I and what river could this be? The Greenbrier River flowed at the end of Big Branch, where our farm was located, but I had spent the night walking *away* from our farm, *away* from the Greenbrier. And now we had come to *another* river? I knew then that Annie and I weren't going to make it home before dawn. I had gotten us more lost than I had ever dreamed possible.

Here comes a truck. I wave the guy down. I don't blame him for being reluctant to stop or for giving me the fish eye when he did stop.

Here I was, a man walking along a highway at 3 a.m. or whatever time it was, leading a horse with a belt around its neck.

I thanked the driver for stopping. "Been trailing this horse all night, got myself lost in a bad way. What river is this? You ever heard of Big Branch Road? That's where I live."

The suspicion in his eyes deepened as if he feared this was the part where I might draw a knife or transfigure into a wolf. "That there is the Greenbrier," he said, indicating the river on the other side of the road. "And about a hundred yards back is Big Branch."

He didn't ask how I could be lost when I was just a hundred yards from the road I live on. He just nodded and left before I could murder him, is what he was probably thinking.

I looked back across the highway at the farm Annie and I had just crept past and saw it for true for the first time tonight, rapidly orienting myself to where I was, everything foreign becoming familiar. The farm was the one my wife and I drove past each time we went to town. The guy who owned it raised cattle on this farm but he and his wife lived in town instead of out here in the country and that's why the house was empty, no dogs in attendance. I hadn't recognized the farm because although I drove past the front of it several times a week, I had never visited the farm or seen the farmhouse from behind, which is how Annie and I originally approached.

What I had done was, I had walked in a wide and all-night circle. You might've read about this phenomenon, how people who are lost in the woods and believe they are walking a straight line sometimes will keep veering off in one direction and eventually walk in a circle that brings them very close to where they started. (One theory is that a dominant leg takes a slightly longer stride which gradually, step-by-step, turns the hiker in a circle.)

I led Annie to Big Branch Road where I met several people who had been called to join the growing crowd at our farmhouse, the searchers gathering there to figure out what to do, where to go, when to strike out looking for me. Someone had a halter, which I put on Annie and then connected a lead rope. A friend asked if I wanted a ride in a truck for the last mile home and let someone else lead the horse. Absolutely not. I've walked this horse all night, I'm walking her home.

At the house, my wife asked, "What happened to you?" She put her arms around me.

"I got lost going after your horse."

She kissed me, wept softly, was happy.

Great stories were told during what was left of that night, large gins were drunk. I said to people over and over, "I thought I was getting more and more lost with each step I took but, turns out, each step was bringing me closer to home."

Between Easter and Christmas of 2003, I lost everything—my marriage, my money, my health, my career, my home, and most terrifying of all, my sanity. The beast that took everything from me was not alcohol or drugs, it was life itself, a potent combination of bad decisions, rotten luck, a debilitating lawsuit, and outlandish adultery . . . eventually involving gunplay, law enforcement, divorce, cancer, and at least one dramatic rush to the emergency room. At a distance of five years, I'm still trying to make sense of what happened. But I know this: the journey of those five years has brought me to a place—where I am now, the people I'm with, what I do, how I view life—that is peace enough and serenity enough to call home. Five years ago I was absolutely convinced that peace and serenity were lost to me forever, but it turns out I was just walking a five-year circle to get home.

PART I

The Things We Push and Pull Through Life

*W*hatever *mental problems* afflicted this homeless guy caused him to engage in bizarre hoarding behavior with two shopping carts. He toured the area around the office where I worked in D.C., pushing one shopping cart, pulling the other, keeping them both filled. I don't mean he filled them the way you might fill a grocery cart in preparation for Thanksgiving, I mean he filled them higher than your head. And stuffed things underneath. And hung bulging plastic bags all around the sides. The carts were as tippingly overfilled as two cartoon carts. Everything relatively neat, though. All the cardboard stuffed under one cart had been folded and stacked with sides aligned. The plastic bags that hung off the sides of the carts had been neatly tied. He had old suitcases and backpacks, brooms and mops, coats, shoes, hats, umbrellas. The stuff was broken, stained, and for the most part unusable, but each item was nonetheless neatly accorded its place on one of the carts.

He was the hardest-working street person I had ever seen. Always packing stuff into, under, onto his two carts. His efforts to move those carts were heartbreaking. Too much stuff. Too heavy. Too top-heavy. He'd trudge down the sidewalk, pushing one cart in front of him and pulling the other behind. The wheels would go screwy and he'd have to stop and align them. Or one of the carts would get stuck in a sidewalk crack. These carts and their wheels were meant for the smooth floors of supermarkets, not sidewalks and curbs. When the double burden became too much, he'd push one cart half a block ahead, then walk back for the second, then push the first another half block. Sometimes stuff would spill and he'd have to repack. Sometimes he'd spot a new treasure—a crate, a piece of plastic—that he would gather up, finding a place for it on the heaps, moving on.

Most tragic of all was watching him cross a busy street. He wouldn't let you help; no one was allowed to touch those carts. But he wanted to get both carts across the street together, afraid I suppose of a light changing and isolating him from one of his carts, half of his possessions on the far side of a busy street. So he'd try to get the carts across in one frantic effort, pushing one, pulling the other, a nervous eye on the traffic light, reaching the curb but then unable to get the carts up the ramp and onto the sidewalk. It wasn't funny. Your heart went out to him and the constant struggle he had arranged for himself with the things he carried and pushed and pulled.

You wanted to ask him, Why are you making all this work for yourself? Or, more cruelly, you might think, if he put that much effort into a real job, he wouldn't be homeless.

I was talking with a friend from work about this guy when the friend said, "I carry around as much stuff as that homeless guy does, except you can't see the things I deal with wherever I go. And if people could see what I carry around, they wouldn't have anything to do with me. You wouldn't be here at lunch with me. The foundation wouldn't employ me. Every day, David. Every place I go. All this *stuff* I carry and push and pull."

He had it right. Some of us, Christ, we're burdened with these goddamn shopping carts so full of stuff it's amazing we can get through the day. All around you, right now, people are pushing and pulling stuff that threatens to tip over and spill at any moment—stuff we have to maneuver across dangerous streets while traffic lights tick down how much time we have left. Stuff that got put in our shopping carts during childhood or by a trauma or by the bad luck of brain chemistry.

In preparation for this book, I talked with people who push and pull a lot of stuff through life: fears, disappointments, self-recriminations. Some of these people are successful with important jobs and major accomplishments—all the more admirable when you consider the stuff they're carrying around while achieving those accomplishments and holding down those jobs. Other people I talked with haven't been so fortunate with their shopping carts, and sometimes they just can't get across the street.

Until I lost everything, I didn't realize how tough life was for so many people. I was arrogant, with little patience for whiners. Suck it up and carry on was my philosophy. But after I got laid low and from the perspective of the dining room floor where I lay sobbing and insane, I eventually realized that some of us can carry a lot and some of us not so much. And it changes at different times of our lives. If your shopping cart is too full, is more than you can maneuver through life, then it's not my place or anyone else's place to say you should've been stronger, been able to carry more.

Something else I discovered: there's a beast out and about and capable of loping into your life, getting you on the ground, and ravaging you. Your beast might be bad luck or cancer or bankruptcy, it might be abandonment by a spouse, the death of a child. People who have not yet encountered the beast are indifferent to its existence, as arrogant as I once was. For them, going to work and dealing with disappointment is as easy as skipping unburdened across a street. Not so easy for others of us who are trying to escape the beast while also pushing and pulling full shopping carts. That's who I'm writing this book for—those of us whose names the beast knows.

KIDNAPPED!

YOU WOULDN'T know this if you've never had alcoholic blackouts but sometimes you snap out of the blackout and *come to* in the middle of an adventure. Maybe it's the fear and adrenaline that kicks your ass out of the blackout and suggests maybe you want to start paying attention. Richard Pryor did a comedy routine on this, coming out of a blackout in the middle of the freeway, driving a hundred miles an hour, suddenly conscious and scared shitless.

My life's first memory begins like that. I remember nothing before the moment that I suddenly acquire memory in the middle of an adventure. It's like tuning in to a radio drama already in progress. I'm in the backseat with my sister, Linda. Linda was two years younger so if I was six, she was four. Mom was driving. She was kidnapping us.

I don't know what issue set off this particular bout of insanity, but as with most of my mother's craziness, the incident was rich with religion. Something about Satan. Something about saving us from hell. I was so young that I don't remember being frightened as much as curious. What the hell was going on? Mom was driving across yards. Cars, including police cars, were following us.

I believe this kidnapping occurred shortly after my younger sister, Nancy, was born. I have two younger sisters. Linda, who died in 1996, and Nancy, who is six years younger than I am. My brother Eric is sixteen years younger than I am, and because I left home when he was still a baby, he and I don't have many shared memories of family life. When our mother kidnapped Linda and me, I remember Nancy being a tiny baby who was left with a grandmother, my father's mother. This was Granite City, Illinois, where my father and his father worked in the steel mills and where I was born and where I, too, would eventually work in those mills.

We're speeding along, the police following at a discreet, non-siren, non-flashing-lights distance, which I know because I occasionally get on my knees and look out the back window—until my mother takes a severe corner and rolls Linda and me along the backseat like two melons out the top of a grocery sack.

Mom eventually pulled across the lawn of a church (I remember the deep gouges the tires left in the grass and thinking someone is going to get in serious trouble) and parked right up against the church building. People appeared. Police stood at a distance, waiting I believe, for the family or the minister to take control of the situation. I think the police mentality was different then. I think back then they didn't feel a need to dominate each situation but sometimes were willing to watch and wait and intervene only as a last measure.

Leaving me and Linda in the car, our mother, screaming about Satan, rushed toward the church doors with the minister following close behind her. Linda looked at me as if I might have an answer. What happened? What do we do now? I didn't know.

Someone took Linda and me into the minister's house, right there next to the church or actually attached to the church. The buildings were red brick. We were led into the kitchen . . . the cleanest, brightest kitchen I had ever seen. I didn't know people kept kitchens like this. I didn't know kitchens were capable of this level of order and cleanliness and operating room brightness. I marveled at floors, clean, and counters, uncluttered, and sinks empty of dirty dishes.

Linda and I were seated at a table. Curious eyes stayed on us as people (neighbors, the minister's family, police, I don't remember, but it seemed a crowd) gathered around to see if we were going to have a breakdown or start speaking in tongues or whatever the spawn of insanity does.

How embarrassed can you be at age six? I remember being absolutely humiliated but resolving not to show any emotion to these gawkers. After a few awkward minutes, everyone was moved out of the kitchen except Linda, me, and the minister's daughter, who might've been nine or ten. She was beautiful. And she was suffused with a saintly empathy for me and my sister, poor little offspring of the crazy woman holed up in the church. Smiling softly, beatifically, the little girl was, I suspect, witnessing for our Lord Jesus Christ. In response to this Christian outpouring, I battened down all my young emotional hatches and let nictitating membranes close over my eyes, determined to show nothing in return for her grace.

She asked if we'd like something to eat. Linda, a bewildered four-year-old, looked again to me for an answer. "No, thank you," I said. How about something to drink? the minister's daughter asked. "How about a nice cold root beer?" I remember Linda looking at me and nodding her head vigorously—she had red curls and freckles and she desperately wanted a root beer.

We didn't have soda in our house, and at age six I'm not sure if I'd ever had a soda, certainly not a root beer, although I had heard tales of just such an elixir: bubbly, sugary, tangy it was rumored to be. Still I declined.

"Are you sure?" the minister's daughter asked sweetly. "We have a bottle right there in the fridge, it won't be any trouble at all."

Linda was now attempting to bypass me, nodding her head at the minister's daughter and reaching her grubby little hand across the table to accept root beer even if it had to be poured into her open palm.

I took Linda's wrist and drew her hand back. "No, thank you," I said on behalf of both of us.

Just about then we heard an ungodly screech and wail. That would be Mom. She either had escaped from the church or had achieved

21

a new level of volume that reached the kitchen. Linda kept looking at me, wondering what we were doing here and when would we be going home and why can't she have root beer. I remember staring straight ahead . . . just . . . waiting . . . for . . . it . . . to . . . be . . . over.

If this happened when Nancy was an infant, then our father had not yet moved us to the farm. We moved to the farm when I was eight; Linda, six; Nancy, two; Eric still eight years from being born. It's important to note the relative date of my first memory of our mother's psychosis because it became family lore that living out on the farm was what drove her crazy, alone all day with infant Nancy as the older kids went to school and my father worked in the steel mills. My mother grew up in a small town with lots of friends and neighbors close by, and she did not like the country, hated being alone. But as my first memory shows, she was crazy before we got to the farm— although I grant that she grew all the crazier being out there with no neighbors in sight, alone with her thoughts day after day, struggling with whatever beast was ravaging her—whatever shopping carts she was desperately pushing and pulling through life—while the rest of us went on blithely with our lives.

I realize, too, that mental illness such as my mother's is in certain aspects like any other disease you're born with, in that my mother did nothing to get it, owes no responsibility for the disease's effects, and is obviously more the victim than any of us who had to deal with the effects of her disease. Her bizarre behavior was simply the result of the disease she had—like having a liver disease that results in jaundice. Would I blame my mother for having hepatitis and yellow skin? Of course not. So I shouldn't blame her for being crazy.

Except hepatitis doesn't cause kidnapping or lead her into my room in the middle of the night when I was twelve years old, waking me with the moon in my window over her shoulder, my mother's face crazy, her eyes wild, telling me in a middle-of-the-night voice that "Daddy's going to kill me—go to sleep now, okay?"

Years ago I read an article about sociopaths who were able to pass themselves off as relatively normal individuals, who made it through life even though they didn't have the usual sympathies and empathies shared by their fellow humans. They passed as normal by learning expected behaviors and suppressing unacceptable behaviors. When witnessing a little doggie running into the street and getting hit by a car, the sociopath's natural reaction might be to bust out laughing but he has learned that such a response would bring him censure from other people, so he reacts instead by faking sympathy, acting distraught.

Similarly, I've learned to display acceptable responses when the topic of mothers comes up. If someone says to me of his or her mother, "I don't know what would've become of me if it hadn't been for my mother, all she sacrificed," I have learned to nod sympathetically instead of scoffing. If someone says, "In a lot of ways, my mother was my best friend," I've learned not to laugh out loud. If someone says he misses his mother, I've learned not to twirl a finger by my ear while crossing my eyes. I'm perfectly safe to be around when mothers are being discussed. I might have no idea what you're talking about but at least I won't say or do something you would find offensive to motherhood.

I read once that Noël Coward so loved his mother that he wrote her a loving and intimate letter each week of his adult life, that they had pet names for each other (Snig and Snoop), and that his mother swooned in her memoir, "No mother ever had such a son."

I have no idea what that's about.

My mother was crazy. Still is, I presume, although she's medicated in a nursing home. Not crazy like Auntie Mame, not eccentric crazy, not wacky crazy, but sadly, bizarrely, destructively, *unentertainingly* crazy.

At some point after the kidnapping, my memory blackout resumed, as it sometimes does with an alcoholic blackout, and I don't recall specifically how the kidnapping ended except that eventually my family members came into the kitchen—I think my aunt Anna May, my father's sister, was among them—to retrieve Linda and me. People were falsely happy in the way adults can be around traumatized children as if a cheery voice and unnaturally widened eyes will convince the children to join in the happiness and forget what little beast had been ravaging them. "Well, *there* you are! Have you two been having fun! Did you get some root beer?" I guess our relatives were told that the kids are safe and sound, in the kitchen having root beer. Linda glaring at me, making it clear that we *could* have had root beer but *the brother* put the kibosh on it.

Later on . . . nothing. No discussion, no reassurances, no explanations. We didn't talk of such things in the family. I suppose we were taken home and life went on. But I can tell you what I *did* with the event. I took it—kidnapped by my mother, humiliated in the preacher's kitchen—and wrapped it in brown paper and tucked it into the bottom of a shopping cart that I would be pushing around the rest of my life.

2

THE OLD MAN

I ALSO HAVE early memories of being awakened in the middle of the night, becoming conscious in midair, flying on the way to my father's shoulders.

Before he moved us to the farm in Mount Olive, Illinois, we lived in a tiny house on Center Street in Granite City, Illinois, the town where the steel mill was located and where I was born. The old man worked swing shift at the mill, and on occasion he would come home from the 3-to-11 shift, rolling in after midnight, not really drunk (alcohol was not one of my father's problems) but definitely jolly— and he would have three or four of his companions with him, and somehow the old man convinced them to come home with him because he wanted to show them his amazing son, Day Mart, which apparently is how I pronounced my name as a toddler.

My father would come into my room and without warning would grab my wrist as I slept and lift me up to his shoulder. It was magical, dreamlike, and it was terrifying to be awakened in flight like that.

He carried me into the kitchen, always the kitchen, where the four other steelworkers were drinking beer, smoking of course, still smelling of the mill even though they always showered after their shift. The old man reminded me to duck as we went down the hallway and under the arch into the living room, and I was carried sleepy-eyed and blinking into that tiny kitchen, a fog of cigarette smoke blurring everything, the room hot from more than a thousand pounds of steelworker flesh, the men grinning and laughing and wet in their eyes.

The old man would grab me off his shoulder the same way he put me up there, one of his meaty paws around my thin wrist, lift and swing, and now I was standing in the middle of the kitchen table—speckled Formica top and aluminum tubes for legs. The men all looking at me with great anticipation from whatever the old man had told them about his amazing five-year-old son. I wore sagging white underwear and an undershirt.

"What's your name, boy?" the old man would bellow.

"Day Mart."

"What're you scared of?"

"Scared of nothin'."

The men all laughed, what a pistol this little Martin kid was, scared of nothin'.

My father instructing me, "Now tell 'em what I taught you."

I took a breath . . . and recited it.

> *You'd scarcely expect,*
> *A boy of my age,*
> *To speak in public,*
> *Upon the stage.*
> *But if I should fall below*
> *The pinnacles of Cicero,*
> *Judge me not with a critic's eye,*
> *But pass my imperfections by.*

Then I'd tell them my name again, "Day Mart," and remind them again what I was scared of: "Scared of nothin'."

They loved it. But they were an easy audience—drunk steelworkers, wicked weary from their shift work, being entertained by a sleepy little boy performing for them like a trained monkey.

And I loved performing for them, I remember that. Big strong workingmen awed by the power of the word, spoken by a child. That too must've had some influence on my becoming a writer.

When my granddaughter, Pearl Lucille, was born on March 14, 2007, just one day after my birthday (there's some debate about whether her mother could've tried harder and had Pearl on my birthday), I researched the saying that my father had taught me and discovered that it was a popular school recitation back in the early years of the twentieth century. I plan to teach it to Pearl. But dragging her out of bed past midnight and putting her on a kitchen table to recite for me and my drunken friends is something that I wouldn't do today. We are careful with our children.

I am, however, grateful for the edges I have from a father who was decidedly not careful with me.

Curtis Charles Martin dropped out of school in sixth grade and worked at various jobs trying to help his family keep body and soul together, a story familiar to millions of poor people during the Great Depression. He joined the Civilian Conservation Corps. He signed up for the Marines when he turned seventeen. Family lore says he joined the Corps a week *before* Pearl Harbor. At an age when most teenage boys are worrying about acne and undoing bra clasps, the old man was making landings in the Pacific theater. The big ones. Iwo Jima and Tarawa. He came through it all, returned home, married a woman he'd met through family connections and with whom he had corresponded throughout the war, got a job as a telephone lineman and then at Granite City Steel, where he would work until his retirement and where his father had worked all *his* life and where I worked briefly before deciding there had to be a less hot way to make a living. I was born thirteen months after they were married; a sister, Linda, followed in two years, another sister, Nancy, four years after that, and then a brother, Eric, came along a lot later, sixteen years after I was born and just two years before I left home.

The old man had two crippling negatives, the way I remember it, but against those two negatives stood an array of positive features that tip the scales in his favor and make me miss him. One negative was a shyness so crippling that I think it prevented him from accomplishing what his talents and intelligence might otherwise have provided. The second negative was rage. But let me start with what the old man had going for him.

He was one of the smartest individuals I've ever known—and this goes beyond simply the stuff he had read or memorized. He was a creative thinker. Made connections not readily apparent to others. If he had been educated and given an opportunity, he might've become a professor.

He was well-read. My lasting memory of my father is of him lying full length on a couch with a paperback in one hand, his glasses up on his forehead, his gaze intent. He was so voracious about knowledge that I think reading was physically thrilling to him. When I came home for visits as a college student, he quizzed me relentlessly about whatever courses I was taking. He knew more about the subjects than I did and expressed contempt for what was being taught—or not being taught—in college.

He loved books and writing. I should say he loved the content of books, not the physical objects. In fact, the old man mangled books. Especially the paperbacks, which made up 90 percent of his books. He folded back the covers to keep the pages open. He subdued books by cracking their spines. And when he wanted to mark a page, he'd lick a thumb and fold down fully half the page. In fact, after the old man finished a book, it looked as if it had been physically attacked, as if the book had resisted giving up its content and the old man had to wrestle and squeeze out the goods.

He wanted to be a writer. I discovered this one summer afternoon snooping in the floored attic that was bedroom to my sisters on one side, me on the other, a chimney and enclosed staircase in the middle. I started sleuthing through a stack of cardboard boxes being stored there in the attic. In one, I found a large envelope from the William Morris Literary Agency. Inside the envelope was a manuscript, my father listed as author, and a rejection letter from the agency. This was an astonishing discovery. *I had never heard a single reference to my father's literary ambitions.* I put some evidence together, however, and realized then why he frequently whispered to my mother about something to do with page after page of his pencil scribblings that she dutifully typed on a manual typewriter. She had worked in a bank and was a good typist. Quietly, secretively, and apparently in fear of being ridiculed for it, the old man was writing a novel.

He wanted to be a writer. This discovery must have had a significant effect on me. The old man, a rough-and-ready ex-Marine, wanting to be a novelist must have legitimized that ambition for me. Made it all right for me to aspire to writing, materialized writing as a possibility.

I found the manuscript when I was a teenager and stupidly did not read it. But I know the book was about me because its title was how I said my name as a toddler. "Day Mart." My father's novel, *Day Mart*.

He loved us. Me, my two sisters, and my younger brother. Loved us passionately, openly, expressively. Whenever the old man greeted me, he would put me in a full body hug, kiss me directly and enthusiastically, and call me darling and honey and baby boy. Especially his baby boy. This continued through the teenage years and into my adulthood. It was sometimes embarrassing in front of others, especially when I was a teenager, but I also felt a secret comfort and joy from being so openly loved by my father. Keep in mind that this was back in the day, and in the working-class environment, when and where expressing love for your children would be considered a little odd, especially a father for his son. Over the years I've talked with my sisters about this and they feel the same way, comforted by an absolute knowledge that our father loved us.

For me, his flaws—terrifying rage and crippling shyness—came out most dramatically after we moved to the farm.

3

MOVING TO THE FARM, WHERE INSANITY ENSUES

EVER SINCE I was old enough to make sense of what the old man was telling me, he talked of buying a ranch where we would raise cattle and hogs and live off the fat of the land. This was *Of Mice and Men* pie in the sky . . . and it turned out to be a disaster on nearly all fronts. But give the old man credit, he actually did it. He bought a farm sixty miles from the mills where he worked and made that brutal round trip every work day. Which is how I came to grow up on a farm.

During that first summer, I was eight, too young to help much as my Father planned to perimeter-fence the farm and run cows and hogs. The new fence was taut, brand-new, red-top woven wire with one strand of barbed wire on top and one on the bottom. Cows wouldn't go over it, hogs couldn't get under it, and neither could go through it. Except the old man never finished fencing the whole place, so our animals would walk along the good fence until they came to the old fence, and then they would get out because the old fence was for shit.

But this was our first summer on the farm and we hadn't had any failures yet. With visions of a complete perimeter fence in his head, the old man hired someone to help cut down trees for fence posts. This was almost like pioneer days, the trees being felled in the forest right next to where the fence was being built. My father and the hired man cut the trunks into eight-foot lengths and then split each length into four triangular fence posts. Although the felling of the big trees and cutting of the trunks was done with a chain saw, the splitting was done with ax and wedge and maul—not that far removed from the way Abe Lincoln did it.

At age eight, I provided support. Run back and get something that had been forgotten. Retrieve a dropped wrench. Fetch water.

The hired man brought along his son who was four years older then me—and meaner than a snake, with all the marks of a future serial killer and arsonist. At the time, though, I thought he was a great companion, old enough to know how the world worked. And he owned a pocketknife—which I coveted and which later that summer played a part in an act of depravity for which I've yet to atone.

The old man, the hired hand, and we two boys are out in the woods on a blazing hot day when the old man tells me, "Go on back to the house and bring us a gallon jug of well water. Make sure you rinse out the jug three times before you fill it." He would've said it, *rench* out the jug.

We used plastic milk jugs to carry water and the old man was fastidious about getting the milk smell out before filling the jugs with water. In fact, he was surprisingly fastidious about a lot of things considering that he worked a filthy job in the mill and his wife, my mother, was a slob who kept a filthy house. I don't know how much of her dirtiness came from being mentally ill and how much was just slovenly habits, but our house was constantly a mess, which they fought about often. One time a neighbor visited when we weren't home, and she looked through the window and saw our kitchen and decided to come on in (doors being unlocked) and do the dishes and clean the house. My mother was livid at this intrusion and had the hardest time figuring out which neighbor lady had done it.

My mother served a meal using the small tinfoil bowls that frozen meat pies came in—to save her from doing dishes and then maybe her husband wouldn't be screaming about piles of unwashed dishes in the sink. When the little tinfoil bowl was set in front of my father, he smelled something bad. The tinfoil apparently hadn't been washed. He lifted it to his face and sniffed again. Shit, I could see it coming. I glanced at my mother and two sisters; they were oblivious. Why couldn't they read the signs, obvious to me, that the volcano was about to blow . . . the old man throwing his tin bowl across the room, splattering a wall. I knew enough to slide a discreet distance from the table because, yes, here he comes around to each of our places, sweeping the little tin bowls onto the floor, my mother weeping piteously, my father screaming about the filth and telling her to clean up this fucking mess.

So I knew enough to rinse the empty milk jug, not just the required three times but four or five or six times because the old man would perform the sniff test before he drank from the plastic jug.

On this particular day, the post splitting was taking place about half a mile from the house. I walked to the farmhouse with the hired man's son. I found an empty milk jug and rinsed it repeatedly before filling it with well water, pressing on the little red cap, and setting off for the two thirsty men in the woods.

A gallon of water weighs about eight pounds, a significant burden for an eight-year-old, especially considering I had to haul that water up and down ravines and cross fences with it and make my way through briars. The older boy never offered to help carry the water and I never thought to ask him. As we finally approached the men—I remember I could see them as they were just lighting up cigarettes to take a break—the older boy said, "Hey let me carry that jug for you a piece." I said, sure, thanks. I'd hefted those eight pounds for half a mile through rough territory and was grateful for the older boy to take the burden these last twenty yards.

We walk in on the men. The older boy says to my father, "Here's your water." I say nothing, not realizing anything was wrong. The old man approached me at a steady pace, Chesterfield hanging from one side of his mouth as it always did. At the mills he had to smoke while his hands were occupied so he learned to light a stubby unfiltered Chesterfield and never touch it again until it was about to burn his lips, at which time he'd shove it out of his mouth with his tongue. When the old man reached me, he hit me so hard with his open hand that he knocked me to the ground—more or less cold-cocked me. I think this was the first time he struck me as opposed to spanking me.

Still unaware of what I'd done wrong, I knew better than to ask.

As I lay there seeing stars and wondering if he was going to hit me again, the old man said, "I told *you* to fetch us that water. Not him, *you*." *Even then*, I thought a terrible mistake had been made. My father was simply unaware that I had in fact carried the water 99.9 percent of the way, that the older boy had simply taken it the last few feet. Any moment now the older boy was going to tell him. And while my father couldn't take back having hit me hard enough to knock me down, at least he'd know I hadn't disobeyed him or shirked my duty. I kept waiting for the older boy to speak. My father handed the water jug to the hired man who said something approving about the way my father had disciplined me, something along the lines of, You gotta keep on 'em when they're young like that or they'll grow up useless to you. When I was able to sit up, I caught the older boy's expression. The bastard was grinning. A mistake had *not* been made—I had been betrayed. This was the first time in my young life that I was even aware of the concept of betrayal, that someone could set you up, could get you in trouble *on purpose,* could arrange to steal credit for something you'd done. It was a lesson hard learned.

I realized then that life on the farm was going to be different from life in Granite City, where all I had to do was get up and go to school, come home and play with the other kids on the block, get home by dark, go to sleep, repeat. Now I had chores, duties, expectations. For whatever I did or failed to do, there would be consequences. It's another lesson you keep learning over and over all your life.

I think it was fairly commonplace back in the day not to discuss things with children. When we moved to the farm, for example, sister Linda and I had no idea what was happening. We were told to get in the car with our grandparents, my father's parents. I don't know where Nancy was, maybe back in Granite City with relatives. Maybe she wasn't coming to the farm until we got indoor plumbing. Linda and I fell asleep on the drive. We woke up at the farm. I'm not even sure if anyone said, "Here's your new home." It was what it was.

The same with routine excursions. One day my mother told me to get the box she'd just used to bring in groceries and take it to the kitchen pantry and put some canned goods in the box. Soup. Also some Quaker oatmeal. That box of saltines. Jar of peanut butter. I had no idea what was going on, if we were preparing a box of food to return to the store and get our money back or what. I didn't ask questions because questions were not entertained. You did what you were told. Asking questions was one step from talking back, which was not only not tolerated but actively punished.

When I finished filling the box, my mother went through it, taking out a few cans and putting them back in the pantry. Then she told me to carry the groceries to the car and get in and ride next to the box so it wouldn't bounce off the seat and spill out on the floor.

I did as I was told. She drove off on whatever mission this was, nothing said to me. As it turned out, we were delivering groceries to a poor family. Desperately poor. I don't know where my mother heard about them, probably from church. No one in the family seemed offended we were bringing food—or particularly grateful, either. They lived in a shack in the woods. Five or six kids all under the age of seven. Looking dull-eyed and only mildly curious at who we were, what we were doing in their home. One room, one sink, one spigot with cold water. The father, a young man not yet thirty, was washing his armpits, grinning at me while my mother talked with his wife about the food we'd brought. The father put on a shirt and slicked back his hair. I think he was heading out for the night. The girls wore dresses, the boys overalls. All were barefoot. Their feet were black. The one-room shack smelled strongly of ammonia from the babies. The inside of this single room had not been dry-walled, so the only barrier to keep out the cold and weather was the lap siding, although someone had begun a systematic but as yet unfinished project to tack flattened cardboard boxes to the inside surface of that lapped siding.

These people were as poor as you can get in America and still be living indoors. This was before food stamps, at least for rural areas, so they survived on handouts and whatever the father made from his unskilled labor. This was a family at risk for malnutrition. The kids either didn't go to school or would soon stop. This was desperation. By comparison, the old man with his steady paycheck from the steel mill made us well off.

Yet my parents argued constantly about money. My father's contention was that she spent too much and was a slob. He would point out that with his last paycheck he brought home however many hundreds of dollars he brought home and now they were broke—where did it go? I could've answered that. The money was spent on the thousand things you have to buy when you're operating an unprofitable farm, on feed and fencing and tools and tires. The old man was as bad a farmer as my mother was a housekeeper.

Still, life proceeded along lines relatively normal for the times. Coming to school with a shiner that your old man gave you hardly made you special in working classes of the late 1950s—and neither did having a mother who was a slob (or, in the case of mothers of friends of mine, secret drinkers or women who had "uncles" come visit while the husband was out of town).

After a few years on the farm, however, our relatively ordinary life turned into a bizarre one that filled those shopping carts I'll be pushing and pulling through the rest of my life. I have to keep in mind that the burden is also a resource, because I draw material from everything that's happened to me. I'm a writer.

My father suffered a growing suspicion that my mother had cheated on him and that my sister Nancy was not his biological child. This suspicion was based partly on looks. I have blue eyes and light brown hair that used to go blond in the summer. My sister Linda had red hair and blue eyes. Nancy has dark hair and brown eyes.

I believe the suspicion was also fueled by my father's disappointments in life—that he was a skilled laborer in a steel mill instead of a writer. I think his crippling shyness prevented him from pursuing his ambitions. He might have been willing to work hard to become a writer, to take classes, certainly to read everything ever written about writing, but he was too utterly, profoundly *embarrassed* to put himself out there and do anything about it. I think disappointment with his life made him vulnerable to anything that showed life was indeed wicked.

He was so shy that he sent me into stores for him. One time when I was nine and my mother's mental illness prevented her from leaving home, the old man took me into town to pick up necessities from the Kroger's on Main Street. I was already accustomed to going into a store to ask directions or take a tractor part in to have it repaired or to do whatever required venturing into a public setting that my father was too shy to face. In the truck outside the Kroger store, he gave me money and said I should go in and ask the lady at the cash register for two things and then she'd go get them for me. At this point I'm not sure if I had ever been in a grocery store, certainly never by myself. "First thing," he said, "is toilet tissue."

I nodded. "Okay, toilet paper."

"*No.* You gotta call it toilet *tissue*, that's how they call it in *polite* society."

I had no idea that something called *polite society* even existed, much less that within that special place different names were given to every-day items. Okay, then. Toilet *tissue*.

"The other thing you got to get is sanitary napkins."

Which I thought was strange because we didn't use napkins in our house. Still, if that's what the old man wanted—and I knew what *sanitary* meant.

"Okay," I told my father. "Toilet tissue and clean napkins."

"No! *Sanitary* napkins, you gotta say it that way so the lady knows what you mean."

But *I* didn't know what I meant. Still, the old man was not to be denied on these matters so I took my skinny nine-year-old ass into the store and walked up to the lady at the cash register and told her I wanted toilet tissue and sanitary napkins. Whenever she asked a question about quantity or size, I gave the same answer, "Just regular." It seemed to work. She put the familiar rolls of toilet paper in a paper bag along with a blue box I had never seen before and gave me my change with a look I had become familiar with by that time, a combination of curiosity and pity.

I never mistook my father's shyness as a sign of his being cowardly or timid. One winter after a massive snowstorm, the old man was driving the whole family into town, being careful because those one-lane country roads were dangerous enough even when there was no snow on the ground and often you crested a hill as an act of faith. At least we thought there would be no one else on the road this particular morning, since the roads were unplowed and covered a foot deep or more with snow.

We were wrong. The old man was taking a corner very slowly when another car swerved toward us, the old man steering our Ford into a ditch to avoid a head-on collision. The other car ended up in a ditch, too.

Normally, the old man might have instructed my mother or me to go talk to the other driver but he was pissed and got out of the car and marched like a Marine through the snow to the other driver. I piled out, too, and followed at a safe distance.

The other driver hadn't exited his car. He was a young man in his mid-twenties, still shaken by the near collision. The old man quietly asks him, "Are you all right?" The man says, Yes, he wasn't hurt. Then the old man asks, "Do you live on this road?" The young man says, No, he lives in town. "What are you doing out here after a snowstorm?" Oh, the kid says, I came out here to shoot my gun. There was a revolver on the front seat next to him.

That's what it took to set the old man off; he pulls open the driver's door, grabs the young man by the collar, and hauls him out in the snow. "You stupid son of a bitch. You nearly wreck my car and kill my family so you can drive out here on these unplowed roads and shoot your gun?" Then the old man marches the kid to our car and demands some paper and a pencil. My mother comes up with a piece of brown paper torn from a grocery bag and a pencil nubbin smaller than the old man's thumb. He hands these items to the kid and orders him to write a confession—that he had no business out here on these unplowed roads, that he was speeding, that he failed to yield right-of-way, basically anything the old man told him to write. Then my father directs the young man to help push our car out of the ditch and we took off, leaving the guy with no help for getting *his* car out of the ditch.

My father drove to a state police substation. I went in with him.

The old man showed the paper-bag confession, signed and dated, to a state trooper and asked if it could be used to have that young man arrested. The trooper didn't think so.

Still, I was amazed at my shy father pulling someone out of his car and entering a state police substation—bold as brass. What else was this man capable of?

Killing my mother. He was most assuredly capable of that because I watched him as he almost did it. My father was driven toward homicide by his suspicion about sister Nancy's paternity, suspicions fueled by her coloring and by his own disappointments in life.

And I have to allow for the possibility that his suspicion was grounded in truth. Strange things occurred in that isolated farmhouse, deep enough in the woods that you couldn't see any neighbors and neighbors couldn't see you. A half-mile lane allowed plenty of time to watch someone approach.

My sister Nancy spent more time in that house with our mother than anyone else. From the time we moved to the farm when Nancy was two until she went to school at age six and a half, she spent every day alone with our crazy mother.

Last year Nancy had a hysterectomy, and after the operation, her doctor asked about the trauma to her uterus. "What trauma?" Nancy asked. The doctor was surprised she didn't know. "It's why you were never able to have children," the doctor explained. "At some point early in your life there was injury to your uterus—bad enough that the scar tissue fused the wall of your uterus to an intestine. That's what we had to deal with during the hysterectomy." Nancy asked what kind of injury the doctor was referring to—some kind of car accident, for example? She had never been in a serious car accident. "No," the doctor told her, "this is the kind of injury we see in sexual abuse cases." *You mean like something stuck up me?* Yes, the doctor said . . . *something like that.*

Nancy told me that she'd always had a *feeling* (she's careful not to call it a memory) that Mom had done something like that to her. In the past, Nancy had dismissed this feeling because she couldn't confirm it with a distinct memory or specific knowledge or evidence of anything like that ever happening. But whenever she saw a movie or read a book about repressed memory or the sexual abuse of a girl by the introduction of foreign objects deeply enough into her vagina to cause injury—she *felt* that something like that had happened to her.

The only thing Nancy and I can conclude for sure is that the anguish in that house was sufficiently bizarre for us to speculate on any variety of things that might have happened.

Nancy also remembers that as a preschooler, she witnessed certain visits from men during the day while my other sister, Linda, and I were at school and our father was at work. Nancy walked into the bathroom during one of these visits and discovered that the visitor, one of our father's friends, had soaped up our mother's legs and was shaving them.

In some families, suspicions continue for a lifetime without resolution. Was the husband carrying on a twenty-year affair with his secretary? Did the wife become impregnated by her husband's brother? People talk. Nothing is ever known for sure.

In our family, however, the pot was boiling and the lid was welded shut and something had to give. The old man's rages became all the more terrible. Our mother's craziness became all the more grotesque. And then the whole thing exploded during one awful night when I was twelve and prevented him, just barely, from killing her.

LIFE GETS WEIRD

I'M ELEVEN, it's winter, after dinner, dark outside, and the old man announces that we're going to put a new head gasket on our ancient Case tractor. My father's work schedule meant that we often ended up doing jobs at odd hours, but this particular night was goddamn cold outside and I knew in my heart that this project wasn't going to end happily. Mainly because he didn't know what he was doing. My father wasn't a mechanic . . . or a farmer. Someone had told him that the tractor needed a new head gasket and sold him one. All he had to do, he was told, was just remove the cylinder head, scrape off the old gasket, put on a new gasket with sealant, put the head back on. We had already taken off the cylinder head and I had scrapped off the old gasket after getting home from school.

My father and I dressed for the cold and marched out to the tractor. Of course we didn't have a garage or shed and worked under a blue tarp that we'd thrown over the tractor. My job was to hold the flashlight and hand my father the tools he needed. A simple task that I would, as usual, somehow screw up.

Because of the cold we did a lousy job of sealing the new gasket. When the old man ran out of sealant, he used a numbed finger to rub some off from where he'd just put it and apply it on down the line. This new head gasket was going to leak, but that's not what worried me at the moment. The current trauma was tightening the bolts, because the old man had a pathological tendency to overtighten bolts. With a cylinder head, this can be especially troublesome because the bolts tighten down into the engine's block and if you overtighten and shear off a bolt, it becomes embedded in the block and has to be drilled out. So I was silently praying that the old man wouldn't overtighten any bolts on this particular night.

Meanwhile, in spite of *wanting* to do my job correctly, on occasion I would let the flashlight's beam wander from the bolt my father was tightening and he would bellow at me to watch what the hell I was doing, all I had to do was hold the light on the work, you'd think even an idiot like me could do that. Then the old man would deliver his judgment of me, a judgment I heard a thousand times growing up. "You're as useless as tits on a boar." Maybe more than a thousand. Let's see . . . twice a week would be a hundred times a year times the ten years I was on the farm with him . . . yeah, a thousand times. More often when I was younger, less so when I grew up, but it averaged out. I later thought if I ever went into therapy and got cured of what ails me, I could have a T-shirt made that would proudly proclaim, "I am MORE useful than tits on a boar!"

As my father tightened each bolt, I'd be thinking, *that's enough, Dad, it's tight enough, don't turn it anymore.* And he'd turn it a little more as I worried that the final half turn would strip the bolt.

He tightened the first three bolts just fine, although I continued bracing myself for the wrench turning freely, which would indicate the bolt had been stripped or sheared. He was snugging down the fourth bolt, giving it that last quarter turn, I was holding my breath wondering if we were going to escape disaster as we had with the first three bolts . . . when his wrench lurched sickeningly and turned freely. *Stripped!*

He looked at me, I refused to look at him. It could go either way. He might just curse and go back to the house. Or his hair-trigger temper could plunge him into a rage. What I found terrifying as a child was not just that he would become so maniacally angry but that his rage would explode so instantaneously.

Jesus Christ, here it comes, I thought. He curses and tosses aside the tarp and swings the adjustable wrench in a wide arc; it goes flying, missing every car and truck window it could have broken and I'm ducking and moving out of reach but he catches me with his boot and, kicked hard in the leg, I fall as he hits me with his open hand on the way down. I remember thinking as I lie balled up there on the frozen ground, Wow, I'm getting through this without really being hurt. I'll have a bruise on my leg, but his other blows landed on a heavy winter coat and now even if he kicks me a few more times, I'm all curled up in a hedgehog ball—that should protect me until his rage dissipates.

He's kicking me and cursing, screaming how it was my fault, that I had one little job to do and failed to do it, I couldn't keep the flashlight on the bolt, no wonder he stripped it, you useless piece of shit, *useless as tits on a boar* . . . I'd rather have one of your sisters out here helping me.

When we worked together and things went wrong, he'd hit me with his hand, with his open hand most often but occasionally with his fist. Kicked me. Hit me with boards or whatever was nearby. Bruised me. Bloodied my nose.

Does it sound strange that I managed to retain affection for my father who knocked me around physically while I have no affection for my mother who never did anything worse than spank me? Her craziness was *humiliating* in ways that the old man's beatings never were—and humiliation and shame take longer to heal. Maybe they never do.

When I was twelve or so, arrangements were made for me to join a bowling team Saturday mornings. Someone would come out to the farm and pick me up and someone would deliver me home again after bowling. At my age and in my circumstances, this bowling arrangement seemed exotic. I suppose I was some do-gooder's civic project. I was the recipient of these projects several times growing up in Mount Olive. A bonus to the bowling project was that the old man was somehow talked into letting me out of farmwork for half of a Saturday.

I had never bowled, but the kids would teach me and I would get socialization and have some fun. About my third Saturday into this social experiment, an adult I didn't know came to me while I was waiting to bowl and said very somberly that I would have to go home now even though we still had a couple games to play. I had learned by this time in my life not to ask why but just to do what I'm told, so I started gathering up my things. But the other kids were curious, a couple of them angry on my behalf. Why does he have to leave? they wanted to know. The adult said, "His mother was just found wandering down Main Street without any clothes on." I wanted to tell the kids who had made inquires on my behalf, See, that's why I don't ask why.

The kids were sympathetic. It's not like in a movie where everyone makes fun of the weird kid. Most of the times when something embarrassing happened related to my mother being crazy, I got sympathy and pity and people wanted to give me a nice cold root beer. Still, the experiences made me a cold fish because I didn't want their goddamn sympathy. As I was leaving the bowling alley, I remained quiet, but inside I was thinking, To hell with all of you and your normal happy lives and cram your pity for me up your happy asses.

Leading up to the terrible night when the old man almost killed her, my mother became increasingly paranoid about exactly that—being murdered by him. She started visiting me late at night, waking me to ask about the old man's plans to bury her body in one of the holes he and I were digging around the farm.

The truth of the holes was almost as bizarre as her speculations. Always scheming to strike it rich, my father got the idea that our hundred acres of scrub farm might contain valuable minerals. What kind, I do not specifically recall, but he spoke often of finding diamonds and claimed he knew someone who found a diamond in Arkansas. Why he would think we might have diamonds on our farm, I have no idea. He wrote away to an obscure state office asking for help determining what minerals, ores, soils were on his property. The office sent a supply of small white cotton canvas bags, each with a card-stock label sewn into a drawstring top, and instructions to fill each bag with the mineral he was interested in having analyzed. He was to keep track of where the sample was found, send the sample off, and a report would be sent back.

For me the best parts of this enterprise were those wonderful little canvas bags with the drawstring closures—they were four or five inches tall and a couple inches wide and stiff when new, but with wear, they became pliable enough for any pocket. Marbles used to come in little bags like that. Tobacco, too. I swiped half a dozen or so from the old man's stash and used them as storage units for my own treasures.

The old man would grab a shovel and give me a mattock and off we'd go into the woods to look for suitable diamond-bearing deposits. I don't think he had any more reason to believe valuable minerals were on the farm than you would have reason to believe that pirate treasure is buried in your yard. In fact, this venture was precisely like you stepping into your backyard and starting to dig for buried treasure that you have absolutely no reason or evidence to believe is there. I'm reminded of the joke about a drunk searching at night under a street light for his car keys. When asked where he lost the keys, the drunk points down the block where there's no streetlight. "If you lost them down there," he is asked, "why are you looking for them here?" The drunk considers this a stupid question. "I'm looking for them here because the light's better here."

So the old man and I are looking for mineral treasure not where such treasure might reasonably exist but where it is convenient for us to search, such as right next to the trail that leads to the back of our forest. We have a routine. With shovel and mattock and a paper sack full of those little canvas bags, their card-stock tags, and a pencil, my father and I would march into the woods on one of his days off. He'd find a suitable spot. His criteria for suitability? I have no idea. Maybe a topographical element or an outcropping or something he smelled or saw. We had more than one dig in progress at any given time, visiting all of them regularly and shoveling out more dirt, picking deeper into the ground to uncover whatever it was we were uncovering.

I'm twelve years old, holding a little canvas bag with an identification card sewn into the top. The old man, waist-deep in a hole, discovers a schmear of something that strikes him as more important, more significant, than plain old dirt. Some kind of clay. Ore? He smells it, rubs it between his fingertips, and then digs out a golf-ball-sized blob of the substance and tells me to bag it. I do so dutifully, writing the time, date, and location—*3rd hole on trail behind pond*. I don't know if he actually ever sent off any of the samples for analysis; if he did, I was never told the results. Still, these were among the more pleasant times we spent together. There were no bolts to overtighten and shear off. The old man was in an expansive mood as he speculated about ceramic clay deposits and the kind of aggregate diamonds are found in. Was he jiving me? Was this his version of a father-son outing? I don't know, but I remember our time digging holes and sampling minerals as a good time.

Good, that is, until Mom started visiting my room to awaken me at 2 a.m. I could hear the old man snoring downstairs, my mother sitting on my bed up in the attic I shared with my sisters—the two of them on one side of the attic, me on the other side, behind the chimney. This was not a second-floor suite, it was an attic that had been floored. When I reached up and touched the slanted ceiling, I was touching the underside of the house's roof. It was murderously hot up there in the summer and freeze-your-ass-off-cold in the winter. Full of wasps, bugs, and the occasional bat. *An attic.*

Two a.m. and I am alerted by my senses that someone is sitting on my bed. I don't remember her waking me, touching me. But I do remember popping my eyes open, the bright moonlit night illuminating her like a ghost. She's staring at me and apparently waiting for me to wake up. And when I do, she asks, "How deep is it?"

"What? How deep is what?"

"The hole."

At first I didn't know what hole she was talking about but then I realized it must be the mineral hole my father and I had been digging earlier that day. How did she even know about it? No one in that family discussed the day's events and I don't remember my mother ever going for walks in the woods. I got the strangest feeling then that she had followed the old man and me that day, keeping to the ridges as we walked the lower trail along the creek—my mad mother slipping from tree trunk to tree trunk to stay hidden from us as she cast down her crazed gaze. Although I have no evidence that she had indeed followed us, she knew about the hole and was demanding of me, "How deep?"

"I don't know. He was standing in the deepest one about up to his waist."

She nodded. "When that hole is deep enough for a body, your father is going to kill me."

I didn't have anything to say to that.

"Kill me and then bury me in that hole," she said by way of explanation as if I was too dense to catch her meaning. "That's what he's digging out there, my grave."

"Minerals," I said. "We're looking for minerals."

"You're looking for what?"

"Diamonds."

She shook her head in pity that her son could be so stupid. "He's digging my grave, and as soon as it's deep enough, your father is going to kill me."

"It's straight down," I countered—meaning that the hole was not horizontal like a grave but was a round hole just wide enough for my father to stand in.

"You think he can't bury me standing up?" she asked contemptuously. Contempt and scorn are the main attitudes I remember my mother striking in response to almost anything her children did or said. She was contemptuous that her kids were so incredibly dumb, lazy, disobedient. And when we tried to please her, she was scornful of our pitiful efforts. One day when I was a teenager, I stopped working in the field because the tractor was overheating. Dirt had clogged the radiator fins, so I shut down the engine and began digging out the dirt with a small screwdriver. My mother came out to see why I wasn't working. I explained about the radiator being clogged. She watched what I was doing for a few minutes, and then said, "For crying out loud, it'll take you all day the way you're picking at it." And with that she took the screwdriver from me and pushed its tip all the way through the radiator, effectively pushing out the dirt but also rupturing one of the cooling tubes positioned between the two layers of cooling fins. Water came out. A lot of it. Green water, tinted as it was with antifreeze, so you know this was something serious. She put her hand over the fins, which of course did nothing to stop the leak. "What are we going to do?" she asked in a panic, knowing the old man would be home in a few hours. I also noted her use of the plural pronoun. She looked at me with crazy eyes and I said, "I could take the radiator off, drive it to town, get them to solder that tube." She wanted to know how much it would cost, and I told her not much, a few dollars—most of the cost was in the time and trouble it would require to remove the radiator, take it to town, have it soldered, get it pressure-tested, bring it home, and reassemble everything, put water and antifreeze back in . . . and as I'm explaining the process, she said scornfully, "Get to it then!" I managed to have it all repaired and put back together before the old man got home, but of course I hadn't had time to finish the field, so he's livid and comes out to the field to tell me, just in case I had briefly forgotten: "You're useless as tits on a boar."

It's 2 a.m. and I'm trying to convince my mother that my father is digging in anticipation of minerals not homicide, but she is scornful of this explanation and says, reasonably as it turns out, "There are no diamonds on this farm. Do you and your father think I'm stupid enough to fall for that? I know exactly why he's digging that hole. You said it's up to his waist?"

"Yeah, about."

She nodded again, apparently satisfied that another three feet of digging had to be completed before her murder would take place. Mom left my bedside as specter-like as she had arrived.

After that, I followed a pattern that continued for several years. Last thing at night, after using the house's only bathroom, which was in the back of my parents' bedroom on the first floor, I would walk through their bedroom, through the living room, and into the kitchen—where I would stop at the knife drawer and take out the largest butcher knife we owned. Then I'd open the door to the attic steps, which were steep and turning and enclosed, and I'd carry that knife to bed, placing it under my pillow in anticipation of another 2 a.m. visit from Mom. First thing in the morning, I'd carry the knife back down and return it to the drawer. Every night, every morning. For years. I was convinced she was crazy enough to kill me or at least show up in the middle of the night at my bedside to do something wacky. And when that shit came down, I wanted to be armed.

She visited me on the grave-hole issue a few more times and, while talking to her, I kept one hand under my pillow and on the knife, which comforted me. No, I would tell her, none of the holes was deep enough to bury anyone in yet.

She was crazy. And yet . . . *and yet* . . . there came the night later that summer when he tried to kill her for real.

5

AWFUL NIGHT NUMBER ONE,
WHEN I WAS TWELVE

I MENTIONED THAT my father had been nursing suspicions about Nancy's paternity. I don't know how long Iago had been whispering poisons in his ear, but the poison and suspicion and rage came out during one awful night the summer after I turned twelve.

We went to a family gathering some forty or so miles from our farm. Something was said there that set my father off, confirming old suspicions he'd been pushing-pulling for months or years that Nancy was not his child. Neither Nancy nor I know for sure what happened to set the old man off.

We speculate that what was said was along the lines of . . . oh, yeah, didn't you know, Charlie (my father's name was Curtis Charles Martin but people called him Charlie), that so-and-so had business that took him near your farm and he used to stop by and visit Margie (my mother, Marjorie Jane Martin) all the time. Well, the old man decidedly did *not* know this. And he must've wondered why my mother *hadn't* told him. A visitor to our farm was a rare event, worth noting. All the more so if that visitor was a man who was with my mother out there in the middle of nowhere, the two of them alone except for the toddler Nancy. In fact, maybe the man was visiting Nancy, his child, who was already two years old when we moved to the farm. The old man must've speculated that these secret farm visits were a continuation of an affair that Mom had started some years before. Issues of paternity and secret liaisons are as old as humankind and as tawdry as tabloid television—but they were about to become astonishingly vivid to our family.

The drive home from the family gathering where the old man had his suspicions confirmed was wild. We would've had a 1958 Ford Galaxie V8 that could haul ass even if it was a family sedan—and the old man was definitely hauling ass home. We were on the famous Route 66, traveling north from the Granite City/St. Louis area. You can drive along that flat straight highway and see to the horizon on both sides of the car.

Our parents were arguing in the front seat while Linda, Nancy, and I rode in the back. Our parents always argued, but this fight was different. The old man's voice seethed; Mom sounded more terrified than I can ever remember. For a distraction, I watched the clouds the way my father had taught me some years before—searching for a peculiar straight-sided mushroom cloud. He was convinced the United States might be bombed on any given day and the first we'd know about it would be seeing a mushroom cloud.

But on this trip home, the war was in the front seat . . . to be continued when we got home, and my father was intent on getting home just as fast as he could. I know we topped a hundred at one point because I dared to peek over the seat to see the speedometer. Mom was sobbing, begging him pitifully, "Charlie, the kids! You'll kill us all." Grim behind that wheel, hunched over it, he was absolutely cold-blooded in his reply: "You're fucking right I'll kill us all."

My sisters were occupied with a quiet game, singing something or patty-caking. They were brilliant at tuning out the drama. During the one family vacation that I can recall us ever taking, we drove out to Yellowstone National Park. It was a disaster on several levels, one being that my mother went darkly crazy on several occasions. Of course the old man hadn't made reservations and was too shy to stop in motels and ask for a room, so once we were in the park, we ended up spending the night in the car. My mother and father spoke urgently through the night—my mother jabbering about being taken by Satan and my father trying to calm her enough that she wouldn't cause a midnight incident that would attract park rangers. My two sisters were asleep in the backseat with me propped up in one corner in absolute misery. At some point in the night, the old man whispered, "David." I considered faking that I was asleep, but I answered him and he said I should quietly get out of the car because he had something to tell me. This can't be good, I thought.

We walked away from the car at 3 a.m. with thoughts of bears vivid in my mind. We had seen a lot of them that day. Do bears come out at night? "You gotta get your sisters to stop singing that song," the old man told me. "It's why your mother is so upset. Or at least it ain't helping matters."

I remembered the song. Nancy and Linda had been singing it for the last five hundred miles. It had an endless variety of stanzas but the refrain was the same:

> *Boom, boom, ain't it great to be crazy*
> *Boom, boom, ain't it great to be nuts*
> *Silly and foolish all day long*
> *Boom, boom, ain't it great to be crazy*

The lyrics might go like this:

> *Way down South where bananas grow*
> *An ant stepped on an elephant's toe.*
> *The elephant said, with tears in his eyes,*
> *Why don't you pick on someone your own size?*

> *Chorus*

> *A horsie and a flea and three blind mice*
> *Sat on a curbstone shooting dice.*

The horsie slipped and fell on the flea.
"Oops," said the flea, "there's a horsie on me."

Over and over they sang it as we drove through America's heartland on the way to Yellowstone, my mother in the front passenger seat wall-eyed with insanity, mumbling crazy shit to the old man about seeing Satan in the crowd of people who'd been waiting at some tourist site, about how we need to love Jesus Christ in case we're all killed in a car accident, rocking back and forth in her seat while the old man gripped the steering wheel, wanting his daughters not to sing about being crazy because it was making their crazy mother all the crazier but fearing to ask them to shut up, because that would acknowledge Mom's craziness, bring it out in the open, force all of us to deal with it.

So I had a talk with my sisters the next day, saying don't sing that song anymore—it bothers Mom.

On our return from the family gathering, Linda and Nancy were playing a distracting game in the backseat while that Ford is blazing down the highway, and I kept searching the clouds, thinking that if one of them was a mushroom cloud, then this hundred-mile-an-hour madness would end and my parents would stop fighting about whatever they were fighting about and we would all have to deal, instead, with a nuclear war. I also wanted a cop to stop us. But my bad luck: no atomic bombs dropped that day, no state trooper pulled us over.

By the time the old man got home, slamming on the brakes, putting the car in a sideways skid, it was a wonder he had not in fact killed us all. We three kids either got sent to bed without supper or were savvy enough to hurry upstairs and get to bed on our own.

I heard my parents arguing. They argued all the time. The old man was always the aggressor, screaming *at* my mother while she sobbed back with explanations, denials, apologies. But this particular night I knew it was something more serious than how my mother could manage to spend my father's entire paycheck with nothing to show for it. For one thing, instead of shouting at her, he was grilling her. I couldn't hear the questions, but I heard her sobbed denials. Then I didn't hear anything for a long time and I fell asleep.

What awoke me was a shout, a cry of anguish, garbled like someone talking through a fan. I thought my parents were arguing outside on the other side of the window fan and I was hearing their voices distorted by the fan blades. I heard it again. Tried to ignore it. Tried to go back to sleep. Again. God, it sounded awful. Not someone arguing. Not just my mother crying. But someone being hurt. Hurt bad.

It went on and on until I had to do something. I crept downstairs. The kitchen lights were on but no one was there. Then I heard it again. Outside. I went to the front door and stepped out into the dark . . . and that's when I saw them.

My mother was flat on her back in the yard, my father astraddle her, his knees pinning her arms to the ground, and he was systematically smashing his fist into her face. She was still wearing the dress-up dress she'd had on for the family function. Sometimes he would hit her and she wouldn't react at all. His rage had finally gone over some edge that he couldn't come back from, and he was intent upon beating her to death. I knew the beating had been going on for some time because I had heard it earlier and tried to ignore it and even fell asleep hearing it.

But now that I was witnessing it, I didn't know what to do. I had seen the old man enraged. I knew that resistance or back talk would only make it worse. Yet my mother was giving no resistance and she was being beaten to death. If I made my presence known, would the old man kill me, too?

Finally, without actually making a conscious decision to do anything, I started screaming at him to stop. I was not a demonstrative kid. This was the first time I had ever shouted at my father.

He stopped hitting her in the face, but he didn't get off her and he didn't turn to look at me—he simply told me to get back to bed. In the past, a direct order from him would have been sufficient; no discussion. But this time I shouted at him again.

That was enough. He got off her and told me, "You little son of a bitch, I will fucking kill you." And then he came for me.

I had never run from my father—but I did now. Some survival instinct told me that while the old man could probably catch me in a straight sprint, he was a top-heavy steelworker and I was a skinny little kid who could zig and zag faster and could keep out of his grasp as long as I kept changing course.

Refusing to engage in an out-and-out chase, he ordered me to stop, but I continued dashing around the yard whenever he approached. The old man couldn't believe this. His wife cheating on him and now his son openly defying him. He again threatened to kill me, but he obviously wasn't going to catch me, so he said that if I would just go back inside the house, he wouldn't hit her again.

"Go on," he said. "It's over. Go back to bed. I can hear your sisters crying, you got them all upset. Go on upstairs and tell them it's okay."

I went inside and opened the attic door and whispered up to Linda and Nancy to be quiet. They weren't about to come downstairs to whatever horror was unfolding but they wanted to know what was wrong. "Dad's beating up on Mom," I told them. "Go on back to bed." They wanted me to come up with them. I said I would. But I had to check on something first.

From the kitchen door, I couldn't hear or see where Mom and Dad had gone so I slipped out the back door and circled around to the front yard. They were gone. I don't remember our dogs being present that night. They were farm dogs, a purebred collie and her half-breed son—Lady and Duke. They lived outside and were always there when you stepped out of the house. But the old man must've locked them in the barn so they wouldn't interfere.

No dogs. No parents. I stood in the yard, listening. I always slept in just my underpants in the summer so that's what I had on. I can remember the gravel hurting my feet when I started walking out the lane.

I hobbled a dozen or so yards down that dusty rocky lane when I saw the old man dragging Mom along by her hair. She was upright and walking, but she was being manhandled. I trailed them, close enough so I could hear what was being said but not so close that the old man had seen me yet.

"You know what I'm going to do to you when I get you down there in those weeds?" the old man asked her in a flat voice, almost matter-of-factly.

She couldn't speak very well, having been battered in the mouth, but she was saying, Yes, she knew what he was going to do to her.

"I'm going to fucking kill you."

"I know," she said.

It seems they had come to an agreement on this issue and now it was simply a matter of consummating the deal.

At the time I didn't think about my mother's earlier worries that Dad had been preparing her grave when he and I were digging for minerals, but she must have had a premonition of this. Maybe it was true about Nancy's paternity and Mom knew the old man was going to find out, and when he did, he would kill her. In fact, maybe digging for minerals really was a subterfuge and the old man had been planning grave sites all along. I have no fucking idea.

They got to the weeds, waist-high, and the old man started to drag her in with him. It was a profane thing to see. I have a sense now that it was like watching a large predator dragging his living prey to a quieter place where the sacrament of death could be played out in privacy—like Grendel dragging a warrior from the great hall to his cave where the devouring can be done at leisure. None of this was going through my young mind at the time, of course—except I did have the strongest sense that a threshold was being crossed; that if my parents went into those weeds, our world would be forever changed.

"Leave her alone!" I shouted. Again, this seemed to arise from my throat without my making a conscious decision to speak.

The old man cursed. Even my mother told me it was okay, I should go back to the house. She knew it was over. He was going to kill her. She'd been expecting it for some time now. It was finally here— terrible in its arrival, but at least the anticipation and worry would at long last end. Forty-five years later I could sympathize with her resignation: almost over, almost done, almost dead.

"Go back home, David," she told me.

But I kept shouting at them. The old man let go of my mother's hair and came for me. He had shoes on and I was barefoot and now I wasn't in the grassy yard where I could outmaneuver him. Here in the road, in the gravel, I wouldn't be able to escape if the old man rushed me. So I kept my distance and let him herd me back to the house. At least we were getting farther away from Mom. If she was smart and still physically able, she'd take off for the woods.

The old man got me back to the house. I went inside. He told me to stay in the goddamn house. "I'm not going to hurt her anymore," he assured me. But I had heard what he'd told her. I had heard the truth in his voice. *I'm going to fucking kill you.*

He waited there a few minutes to see if I was going to stay put, then went back down the lane. But I went back after them again, pausing to put on a pair of shoes, no socks, both sisters weeping inconsolably and asking me what was wrong, why was he hitting her, and—tellingly—*what had she done.*

The old man was almost to my mother, who was stupidly still sitting there by the side of the road waiting for her fate to be delivered. When I caught up, I told him again, "Leave her alone!"

"Okay," he finally said. "I'm taking her back and we're going to sit in the kitchen."

This time I could hear the resignation in his voice, *he's not going to kill her,* and I believed him.

I backtracked to the house, waiting for both of them to enter. My mother's face was awful. She seemed stunned, zombie-like. He sat her at the kitchen table and told me I could go upstairs now and go back to sleep, it was over. "Tell your sisters everything is okay." They were still crying.

"I'll stay here in the kitchen with you."

I don't know where this rebellion was coming from.

"You'll go to bed like I told you!"

When he came toward me, I opened the attic door and went halfway up the steps. More exasperated now than enraged, he told me, "Now stay up here, damn it!"

From the top of the steps, I picked up Linda's baton from her twirling class and followed the old man back down the steps. Hearing me behind him, he turned and I lifted the baton over my head to hit him.

It must've seemed funny to the old man at some level. He had a sense of humor that would've appreciated the scene if he had not been *in* the scene. This skinny twelve-year-old kid in his underpants . . . so skinny that he was always making me milk shakes into which he broke two or three raw eggs in an effort to help me put on weight . . . his skinny son holding a glittery baton and threatening to strike a blow for crazy old philandering Mom.

I feigned hitting him and he drew back. He started to say something about how if I hit him he'd kill me, but I guess there had been enough homicide talk that night because all he got out was "If you dare to hit me with that . . ."

He finally surrendered to the ridiculousness of the situation and went to the kitchen where Mom was sitting, dazed, and I followed him down.

They sat across from each other at the kitchen table. Maybe it was the same one on which he had deposited me to recite my "You'd scarcely expect a boy of my age . . ." speech. My mother was weeping pitifully. The old man was grim.

Incredibly, I began lecturing them, telling my parents they had so much to be grateful for . . . look, there's a brand-new chest-type deep freeze and all these other appliances and this house and the farm. Anything that popped into my head. Three kids. A car. A pickup truck. Tractor. Such a rich life, I suppose I was saying, that you have no reason to be fussing with each other. Even at the time I realized it was awkward and pointless and embarrassing. But for some reason the old man didn't try to stop me. And Mom just kept crying. I guess they were both exhausted. Letting me spout off was easier than summoning the energy to get me out of that kitchen and up to the attic.

The awful night petered out after that. The old man went to bed. Mom put her head down on the table and wept, staying there, I suppose, until morning. I went upstairs to give a report to my sisters, but they were in the same bed together, sleeping.

The next day, Dad put Mom on a Greyhound bus and told her to get the fuck out of his life, he didn't care where she went or what she did—he never wanted to see her again. She insisted on taking Nancy with her, my mother convinced that dad would harm Nancy for not being his. And just to make the ironies and dramas all the richer, our sister Linda said years later that she hated Nancy for having been cho-sen by our mother while Linda, the other girl in the family, was left behind with Dad and David.

It's not true that Dad would've hurt Nancy for not being his. He adored her as much as, if not more than, the rest of the kids—after all, she was the baby of the family for ten years until Eric was born. Nancy is clear on this point, that she never felt slighted or unloved by the old man.

Linda and I got ourselves off to school that next morning. Of course we didn't tell anyone at school what had happened—we kept everything about our family secret from outsiders. When we got home, no one was there. I did my chores and Linda, ten years old, made us Campbell's soup for supper. I don't remember that we dis-cussed what had happened but I suppose we must have speculated on what might become of us if neither of our parents ever returned, how long could we make it on our own, when would we have to tell some-one, and who would we tell? But the old man came home from the day shift like usual and told us that Mom and Nancy would be gone for a while. "How long?" Linda asked. Dad said he wasn't sure. Mean-while, we'd have to help out around the house, get ourselves off to school; a neighbor lady would be coming over afternoons so we'd have someone there when we got home, someone to make dinner.

The old man always went to bed early because when he was on the day shift he got up at 4:30 a.m. to make the trip to work. When I could hear him snoring I came down from the attic, found a flashlight, and took the dogs with me out into the woods. I checked all our min-eral holes. Mom wasn't in any of them.

And here's another reason I had to write this book to make sense of my life: forty-five years after that awful night, I relived it. I played my father's part, cuckolded and enraged. I also played my mother's part, crazy as a loon. I had to write this book to understand how I could have made so little progress in forty-five years.

6

AFTER THAT AWFUL NIGHT

AFTER THAT awful night, our lives became a series of disruptions. We were shunted off temporarily to various relatives and sometimes I'd return home to live there alone while the old man was at work and I could catch up on chores. One time my mother arrived driving a Buick (but without Nancy). I told her I was happy to see her, not mentioning the bruises and black eye she still had. I said something about her car. "Wow, you bought a Buick." Her reply came back with the usual contempt she had for her children. "Don't be an idiot, this is your Aunt Evelyn's car." Of course. I should've known that. "How would I afford to buy a car?" she added. Of course. She had no money, no job, no prospects. It was an insight into why she eventually returned to my father in spite of what he'd done to her.

When my mother and Nancy did return that fall and we were together again as a family, the old man was chastened. I think he had been subdued by a consideration of what he was capable of doing. That night showed him where his rages could carry him: to murder. He started going to church. He gave up his beloved Chesterfields. And he didn't fly into rages as often, as deeply. Eventually, after I turned eighteen and left home, he lived like an old warrior with all his battles behind him.

Not to say he was devoid of piss and vinegar. When my little brother, Eric, was seven years old and acting, by his own admission, like a total out-of-control brat, my father did not strike him or fly into a rage as he would've done in the old days. Instead he tied Eric to a chair with duct tape and then placed the chair on the shoulder of the highway—old Route 66—with a sign that said, "Boy for sale." I *think* the old man waited in a safe place to ensure that no harm came to my brother, but we don't know for sure. Eric said he seriously thought someone might stop and cart him away.

In the six years from that terrible night until I left home, while Dad was acting like a better man, Mom got worse. She had been away, staying with her sister, for several months after the beating and then came home and went bat-shit crazy in new and more bizarre ways. Ended up naked in town and other shit, repeatedly daring the old man to complete the threat he had made that terrible night, to go ahead and kill her—and if he didn't, he was chickenshit.

A few months after she returned home following the beating, she came back from grocery shopping three hours late. The old man was in the living room reading, I was on the couch pretending to sleep, and here was Mom coming in with a crazy, defiant attitude. I peeked. I saw the way she stood there smirking, her legs apart. She'd always been meek toward my father, avoiding a direct stare, assuming the body language of submission, but now she was trying to goad him.

Dad asked, rather gently I thought, where had she been and was everything okay—he'd been worried. She said, "I walked into Pitz's Place and told 'em I was going to fuck every man in that tavern . . . and this is how long it took me to do it." In the old days, my father would have knocked her to the ground but now, the newly subdued him just shook his head at what he had wrought.

He knew she'd gone mad and that he'd played his part in having delivered her there. Eventually, when she got crazy-bad, he dropped the girls off with a neighbor and took me along for a trip to the Jacksonville state mental asylum. Considering his pathological shyness, I can't imagine the fortitude it took for him to drive to a mental hospital, walk in, and ask for treatment for my mother. He must've sucked it up and, mortified, told the first staff person he came to, *My wife's in the car and she's crazy.*

I was fourteen then and despised her for this sickness. Because her affliction manifested itself in behavior and because that behavior seemed willful, I was convinced that she acted crazy on purpose—that she could stop anytime she wanted to, really wanted to. The fact that she didn't stop meant that she was hateful. I had no sympathy for her. She was an utter embarrassment to me.

At the Jacksonville mental hospital, I was assigned to stay in the car and make sure she didn't escape or hurt herself. During this long afternoon wait for the old man to emerge with some answer about what we were going to do with her . . . my mother tried to get me to have sex with her. We were in the backseat of the Ford where Dad made Mom ride so she couldn't grab the steering wheel while he drove. My job on the trip to Jacksonville was to ride in the back and prevent her from opening a door and jumping out. So now we're on the campus of the state mental asylum and Mom has worked her way off the rear seat onto the floor and she's talking about God and Satan and hell and how someone/something is going to kill her.

"You can screw me," she said. She was half sitting on the floor and had pulled up her dress to reveal her white underwear with the crotch a darker shade of white. I had never seen women's underwear actually *on* a woman. "Hurry up, you can screw me before your father gets back."

She reached for me, wanting to pull me on top of her. At *fourteen*, I was soaked in testosterone, constantly erect, a compulsive masturbator. I can do this, I'm thinking. I can close my eyes and pretend she's someone from my class at school—but then she grasped me with her clammy insane hands and tried to pull me down, and I recoiled.

I pushed my way out of the car, standing there with a profane erection.

Dad hadn't returned. How many hours does it take to get someone committed? I found a park bench near where our car was parked and sat there, keeping an eye on the car door. When Mom finally stepped out, I went over and led her to the bench. We sat there in the lengthening afternoon. The asylum's parklike grounds had many large trees on a rolling landscape. Mom babbled softly. A young man came over. He was African American, in his late teens or early twenties. I had no way of knowing if he was a patient or visitor.

He had a large egg in his right hand, a goose egg or duck egg. He said, "This is the toughest egg in the world. You can't break it." I nodded, thinking, okay, he's a patient. He tried to hand me the egg. I refused it. He insisted, saying, *Go on, just try to break it.* I could tell he wasn't going to leave us alone until I tried to break the egg, and I was worried that he would become agitated—so I took the egg from him, figuring maybe it was ceramic or painted wood and that was the joke. But I had handled enough eggs to know by the heft and feel that it was real. He said I should interlace my fingers and put the egg in my palm and try to break it but, don't worry, it was the toughest egg in the world and I wouldn't be able to. I was afraid of the consequences of breaking this crazy man's egg. I put the egg between my two hands and *pretended* to squeeze, grimacing as if I was squeezing with all my might. Then I handed the egg back. He seemed satisfied, perhaps a little surprised, and went on his way.

I don't think my mother noticed any of it, sitting on her end of the bench weeping and mumbling and insane.

Dad eventually got her committed. Over the next year or so, she went through extreme therapies that included being wrapped in wet sheets and immersed in water, electroshock therapy, insulin shock therapy, and I think she might've been a candidate for a lobotomy, but even then lobotomies were going out of fashion. The only thing that worked eventually and continuously was some combination of powerful psychotropic drugs that the pharmaceutical industry developed in the 1960s.

Which is how my mother eventually got her insanity under control, no longer crazy or at least no longer acting crazy—and in the end, unfortunately, that's all we cared about, that she was no longer an embarrassment to us. I pity her for the torture that life put her through.

When I lost everything five years ago, I was immersed in mental anguish for six months and spent a year recovering from it. I can't imagine the sustained horror of being crazy like that for most of your life. I am sorry I wasn't able to be more sympathetic to her. I am sorry I didn't appreciate that the contempt and scorn and coldness she expressed toward her kids were symptoms of her disease. I should have told her I loved her . . . even if I didn't or even if she didn't want to hear it. She's still alive but is in and out of awareness. And, in that place in most people's hearts where love for mother exists, I still feel nothing. I'm sorry, Mom.

PART II

Who's Driving This Life?

imagine that in my head there's a control room, something like the flight deck of a starship—the type you've seen in space movies. Dominating the front is a large screen that shows what your eyes see. Speakers play what you hear. Various other sensors record what you taste, what hurts, what feels good, whether you're cold or hot or just right, and there are even panic alarms that go off with sirens and whistles and lights if you're terrified, in fear of your life, ready to flee or to fight to the death. This main front-of-the-room control function is operated by the External Reality Team. These individuals are (for the most part) well-coordinated, conscientious, competent, and pretty much all business. I think of them as serious men and women wearing crisp uniforms and performing in the manner of competent, if soulless, corporate executives. They handle what comes along. You're driving a car, writing a report, delivering a speech, kissing a lover—whatever has to be done, the External Reality Team is in charge. You hear something funny, and the team member in charge of humor hits the appropriate responses and you laugh. But if you laugh too hard, the team is ready to throttle back and prevent you from embarrassing yourself. All is handled relatively smoothly. Such is how we deal with reality.

Usually the External Reality Team members talk with each other and work well together to handle routine matters and crises. Someone bumps into you and spills hot coffee on your tan trousers. The team member in charge of anger is ready to curse the guy, but the other team members are monitoring the situation and offer a constant flow of recommendations. "It's a public place." "Some of your coworkers are here, how's it going to reflect on you back at the office if you curse this guy?" "Look at his face, he's clearly sorry." "It was an accident."

When you go to sleep, the team rests, keeping a couple members catnapping at the controls so they can wake up and go into action if something happens that requires conscious control.

While the coordinated, reasoned, sane, and sober External Reality Team is at the controls, driving your life, there's another group in your mind, lurking in the back of the room. These individuals are more interesting perhaps than the External Reality Team but more messed up, too. I see them sitting in a semicircular row of folding chairs at the back of the control room. They're wearing jeans and sweaters with holes in them or old tweed jackets and khaki pants with unfortunate stains or faded housedresses. Some of these guys and gals have tics and some are close to tears and others haven't slept for days while some are boiling with anger as others cower in a corner paralyzed with fear. Some of these guys are talking to one another or to themselves. Their influence comes from the advice or demands they shout to the External Reality Team. Rules say that these guys must stay in their chairs at the back of the room and not approach the controls in the front— they are too intemperate to be in charge of anything. The Guys in the Back Row don't always follow the rules, however.

Some of the Guys in the Back Row are in charge of your memories—not necessarily the jolly, holly memories of happy Christmases past, not the memory of how to get to the parkway from your friend's house. The Guys in the Back Row are in charge of your deep, dark memories that the External Reality Team would just as soon not be reminded of.

Others of the Guys in the Back Row are in charge of deep impulses. Sexual ones. And impulses that are bound to your fears, your rage, your base desires. Some are morose, living a constant pity party, while a few have stars in their eyes and believe that some good will come from even the most horrible of situations.

But the Guys in the Back Row represent more than just our unbridled id. Some of them are in possession of intimate knowledge about what we *really* want, as opposed to how our External Reality Team interprets what we think we want, or what we're supposed to want according to society, friends, parents, spouses.

Because the Guys in the Back Row are not allowed to touch the controls, when they watch us making a life decision that is contrary to what they think we really, truly want deep in our unconscious soul or when they see or hear something that reminds them of a long-suppressed memory—all they can do is shout at the External Reality Team, which ignores them as best it can.

The primary dynamic between the two groups is that the External Reality Team considers the Guys in the Back Row as illogical, ruled by their emotions, and crippled by tics, phobias, and hang-ups. The main charge that the Guys in the Back Row levy against External Reality Team members is that they simply do not get it. They're in control, they blithely go through life one day after the next, but they aren't in touch with what we really want, really need, what really makes us tick.

When I was fourteen and my mother tried to get me to have sex with her in the car parked on the grounds of the asylum in Jacksonville, Illinois, the External Reality Team made the right decision, of course, but that decision was reached over the screaming, slobbering, half-mad Guy in the Back Row who represented pure sexual arousal. The idea that we could get laid, right there, right now . . . he was astonished and outraged that we would turn down the opportunity.

But it's my mother.

Mother-schmother . . . it's a piece of ass, he was screaming—and we have not yet had a piece of ass, he points out, even though we've been waking up with raging hard-ons for a couple years now and compulsively masturbating and hobbling around at school with erections so embarrassing we can't stand up to answer a question in class and all the girls look delicious, as do the teachers . . . *let's do it.*

We didn't do it and he thought we were a chump for passing it up.

You can hardly blame this sex Guy in the Back Row, he was receiving a daily dose of a powerful drug—testosterone. And it made him crazy. Made him make me all hard all the time. In his drug-induced sexual craze, he suggested bizarre scenarios to me on a daily basis . . . hourly basis . . . every few minutes. We could fuck our teacher. We could fuck the fat neighbor girl. We could fuck the dog. A pig. A pillow. Women sometimes think this adolescent male focus on sex is disgusting and pitiful. These people who are women think that we males should be able to control our behavior, just as I thought my insane mother should be able to control hers. But these people who are women do not fully appreciate the physical effects of receiving a continuous dose of a powerful drug that alters the way you think and behave. When studies find that adolescent boys and young men think about sex on the order of once every fifteen seconds during their entire waking lives, do you people who are women wonder why that is . . . do you speculate that it is our willful behavior and that these boys and men could be thinking about puppy dogs or restaurant selection if they wanted to? No. If you receive a powerful diuretic, you are forced to pee despite the embarrassment of being caught short. Boys and men receiving testosterone are forced to focus on sex. The best we can hope for is that these boys and men will have an External Reality Team sufficiently in control to prevent the testosterone victims from doing hurtful things to themselves and, especially, to other people including most especially those people who are women.

The drug dose that makes the sex Guy in the Back Row crazy is especially powerful when the male is in his teens and into his twenties and thirties, but then, thank God, the dosage begins to decline and the sex Guy in the Back Row doesn't shout so loudly anymore, his demands for action are made more matter-of-factly, and our take on sexual matters can be put into perspective. As I got older and my sex Guy in the Back Row became more reasonable, I began to think more like a woman and appreciate why they so often have the upper hand in these matters—undrugged as they are and able to calculate with a relatively clear head.

As I tried to make sense of why I lost everything, an analysis of the interplay between the External Reality Team (in control) and the Guys in the Back Row (trying to shout advice—not always *good* advice—from the deeper recesses of our mind)—proved useful.

For example, I usually feel comfortable speaking in public but recently I froze at work during a diversity meeting where each person was asked to give a short biographical sketch of his or her childhood. When I started speaking about my father, my throat closed and my voice broke and I could barely choke out the sentences. This was at a *business* meeting. Although this reaction was inexplicable to me at the time, I later speculated that while the External Reality Team was preparing a reasoned public discourse, one of the Guys in the Back Row started wailing about Daddy, how he used to beat the snot out of me, but how he loved me, too, and called me his baby boy before knocking me to the ground, kicking me with a booted foot . . . boo-hoo, Daddy, I hate you, Daddy, I love you, Daddy, I miss you . . . the Guy in the Back Row producing such an Irish-wake racket that the External Reality Team became a discombobulated, stammering, mess.

And I think the interplay between the Guys in the Back Row and the External Reality Team also gives me insight into my mother's behavior. Some years ago, after being managed by powerful drugs for decades, my mother stopped taking those drugs and dipped quickly back into madness. My sister, Linda, was called to help our father get Mom out of a church she had holed up in. The doctor later explained it wasn't that unusual for psychiatric patients to feel so good and normal that they think they must be cured and no longer need their drugs, not appreciating that it's the drugs making them feel normal. Mom went back on the drugs and was okay. Telling me about this episode, Linda asked, "Do you remember how Mom would occasionally catch your eye during one of her crazy episodes and wink and smile like the whole thing was a put-on?" The hair on my arms stood up when Linda said this because I remembered with an awful clarity that sly look Mom would get in the middle of the chaos her madness was causing. That wink and grin was one reason we sometimes thought her madness was simply willful behavior.

But I have another take on it now. Imagine that her crazy Guys in the Back Row have bulled their way forward, have taken over complete control, and now every crazy statement, impulse, random insane act—all of it gets played out because the Guys in the Back Row have pushed the External Reality Team to the side. But the conscientious External Reality Team is not completely without influence and when, during one of these episodes, they saw us kids sitting there mortified with embarrassment or terrified about what might happen next with a crazy mother, the External Reality Team, in a reversal of the usual procedure, shouted to the Guys in the Back Row, convincing them to do something for the kids, for crying out loud. Smile at them, wink at them, give the poor little bastards some indication that this isn't the end of the world. Of course, the kind of grin and wink that the Guys in the Back Row were able to produce was blood-chilling in its creepiness, but still, I think the impulse arose from a good place and simply got fucked up in the translation.

All the time I was growing up, until I left home and began working in the steel mill at age eighteen, my Guys in the Back Row were emotional messes about sex, about fear, yearnings, embarrassments, ambitions, anger, revenge. Probably not that different from your Guys in the Back Row. Then, at the mill, I began drinking alcohol for the first time and added intoxication to the mix. My Guys in the Back Row, like yours, were already a dangerous, unpredictable, occasionally pathetic lot. Drunk, they became nuttier and more entertaining and, as incorrect as it is to say this, it was my Guys in the Back Row being drunk that enabled me to *become* a writer.

7

I WISH I HAD DRUNK MORE GIN

THIS IS going to piss off a lot of people. People who think I should be deeply ashamed about the gin I did drink and specifically apologetic to them for what I said while under its influence, who believe I should be just as sorry as I can possibly be for the way I behaved over the years while drinking gin. And I am. I'm sorry. Really, I am sorry. But let me plead my case for gin.

My Childhood, a portion of which has been described in these pages, was funneling me toward an adult reality—to be clinically shy like my father and crazy like my mother. I'm not saying that gin saved my life, but I am saying that, without the gin dreams of being a writer, I might never have become a writer. And without the courage of gin, I never would have gone into journalism instead of medicine, which is what my father wanted for me . . . but I told him, you know, Dad, you and Mom aren't paying a fucking dollar for my schooling now. I'm paying it all, taking out loans, working two jobs, washing dishes at a fucking fraternity so I can steal uneaten pork chops off the plates of rich snots, and all of that doesn't leave you with much say in the matter . . . the gin and I told the old man this via phone because, even drunk, I would not have had the courage to talk to him like that in person. Without the gin I probably would have become a psychologist. That was my course of study when I enrolled at the University of Illinois. Psychology. Of course. Craziness was the family business.

Writing is what I wanted to do, writer is what I wanted to be— these ambitions starting at age fourteen when I wrote a story about a giant catfish and the boy who spent an entire summer trying to catch the fish, *anticipating Moby Dick*, which I had not yet read. And the teacher kept me after school to find out where I had copied the story from. I told her I didn't copy it, I made it up. She said she'd been grading papers for thirty years and she knew the difference between a student's story and a story the student had stolen from a published book. I said again that I didn't copy it, I made it up, and something about the genuineness of my assertion apparently convinced her not to pursue the matter. I remember walking home from the school bus, a dreamy walk down our half-mile dusty lane, ecstatic that the teacher thought the story was good enough to have been stolen from a published source.

I loved the stories my father and his steel-mill buddies and the local farmers told. Storytelling was commonplace back in the day. I promised myself I would write stories the rest of my life.

How many gallons of gin did it take for that promise to come true?

Maybe I would've written stories all my life even without the gin but I wouldn't *have become a writer* and wouldn't have had the panache to believe I could be published and then to act upon that belief. My manuscripts would've accumulated in the attic with my father's unpublished novel, *Day Mart*.

To explain how the gin worked its way on me, I have to start with beer because beer is what I started with, after hours at the steel mill where I jackhammered slag out of open-hearth furnaces, wearing wooden soles strapped onto my boots because otherwise the heat from the slag would've burned through my boots and blistered my feet. When the open-hearth furnaces were shut down to be re-bricked, we lowly laborers went in to jackhammer the remaining slag so the old bricks could be knocked out. Some of that slag was still glowing red. We wore asbestos. It was the hottest work I'd ever done in my life. You could work inside the furnace for a maximum of fifteen minutes. Then you'd recycle out and drink as much water as you could, then back in. There were always stories about laborers who collapsed from the heat, fell into the red hot slag, and were burned to death. I never saw it, though.

I was one of those hardworking farm kids who came to town for union wages. The mills loved us. We'd been accustomed to hard, hot work all our lives, and the idea of getting paid, instead of getting cuffed around by the old man, and putting in *only* eight hours a day instead of sunup to sundown made the mills seem easy by comparison. My father used to tell me, "Give a man nine hours' work for eight hours' pay and you'll always have a job." The old man also told me something that I used in my novel, *Crazy Love*: "You might not be the smartest guy on the job or the richest—but by God you can outwork all those bastards."

Chores at dawn before school and chores until dark after school. Then putting up hay in the summer, which had been the hottest work I ever did until I got to the mills. If we ran low on work, the old man would hire me out to other farmers. One summer when I was fifteen, a farmer hired me to chop beans. He was growing soybeans in a field where, the previous year, he had grown corn. Some of that corn had dropped its seed, which had sprouted among the beans. We called it volunteer corn, and whatever was growing within the rows of beans had to be chopped out by hand; otherwise, not only would it suck nutrients away from the beans, but the stalks would mess up the combine when the beans were harvested.

The farmer came to get me late morning because if you started at dawn, as we did with most jobs, the dew on the bushy, waist-high beans would have you soaking wet after the first few rows. In his truck was a milk jug of well water and a machete. He asked me if I knew how to chop beans. I said I did. The field I had chopped on our farm was about three acres. This farmer drove me to a field that seemed to stretch to the horizon. Twenty acres? A hundred and twenty acres? It was heartbreakingly large.

He dropped me off at the edge of this infinite field of beans and set out the water, handed me the machete. He said he had sharpened the machete just that morning and it should keep its edge all day if I didn't fool around and hit it into the dirt. He said I should remember to keep moving the water jug, row by row, because I'd be needing every drop of it before the day was out. I still couldn't get over the sweeping size of this field and finally asked him, "Am I going to chop this whole field?"

He said, "You are. One row at a time, son—one row at a time."

Without gin, one row at a time is how I would have lived my life. Steel mill, college, job, marriage, kids, retirement, getting fat, watching television, dying of diabetic complications. *Except . . .*

Beer intervened. That first summer in the mills, where I worked after high school and between college semesters, instead of going home after the shift, eating supper, watching television, going to bed, getting up for the next day's shift—one row at a time—I was introduced to beer.

A joint across the street from the entrance to the mill had a chest-type deep freeze along one wall, and in that freezer were frosted mugs—mugs that had been put into the freezer wet so that the water froze around the glass. And you'd go in this bar on a blazing hot summer's day after spending eight hours in the furnaces and hope to God that there were still frosted mugs left, take one out, walk it to the barmaid, and she'd draw you an icy cold one. I would write sonnets to that beer.

The painfully shy, backward farm boy found himself able to joke with the steelworkers, make them laugh, tell stories that were in my head but had never before been given voice. Liberation! I don't know what would have become of me if I and beer had never liberated that story-telling voice that sat in the back row with the other Guys in the Back Row, quietly mumbling stories of hogs swimming under ice and giant catfish and the courage it takes to sleep with a knife under your pillow.

A *healthier* and more socially acceptable way for me to have liberated my writing voice would have been to find a kindly writing teacher to take me under her wing and light the way to self-awareness with her knowledge and understanding . . . but it happened with booze. In fact, later on, the man who would teach me more about writing, who would instill within me a lifelong appreciation and discernment of the subtlety and precision of words, was an alcoholic who also introduced me to a life of regular drinking.

Once I started drinking beer, my life changed. Instead of one row at a time, working, eating, watching television, sleeping, working—I would drink beer and travel from bar to bar after my shifts. For the first time in my obedient life, I started getting into trouble as the Guys in the Back Row, emboldened by alcohol, would occasionally rush the External Reality Team and take over, causing us to do mad and foolish and illegal things. My use of alcohol almost derailed plans for my first marriage. But I didn't drink *enough*.

The afternoon shift, three to eleven, we called it, wasn't so bad on health and well-being because we could hit the bars and nightclubs before midnight and stay drinking until they closed at 2 or 3 a.m. and then get home, get a full sleep, and still get up in time for work in the early afternoon (factoring in an hour's commute).

Working days, from 7 a.m. to 3 p.m., was brutal because we'd come home, take a nap, then *still* close the bars at 2 or 3 in the morning, then go to work suffering a combination of hangover and intoxication and total exhaustion. We carpooled, and when it was my turn to drive, more than once I fell into a kind of half-awake, half-asleep zombie state that somehow allowed me to drive sixty miles to work without remembering much about the trip until I pulled into the mill's graveled parking lot. The highways were especially empty at dawn, and I suppose I knew the route so well that I drove on automatic pilot. The External Reality Team, seeing all the crazy Guys in the Back Row passed out, must have stepped up, taken responsibility, and got us to work. One morning the father of a girl I was dating and would eventually marry passed the car I was driving, later giving his daughter an outraged report about what he'd seen. "Four of them in the car. Two in the back, two in the front. *All four of them asleep, including your boyfriend, who was driving*! He had his head leaned against the side window and his eyes might've been open, but I drove parallel to them a mile or so and I'm telling you, he was asleep! Until I honked my horn."

Thank you, Baby Jesus, for not letting me crash and kill or maim myself and my friends and any number of innocent bystanders during all the times I drove asleep, hung over, wasted, drunk, and generally having no business behind a wheel. Now I won't drive if I've had even a single glass of wine—Baby Jesus is a loving and tolerant God, but even He eventually leaves you to your fate.

If I had not started drinking beer and if alcohol had not had its liberating effect on me, if in fact I had not had an obsessive-compulsive personality, I would have missed out on adventures that have informed my writing and life ever since.

I was eighteen with mill money in my pocket, I was James Dean going to the jazz joints and nightclubs and hootchie places in East St. Louis. East St. Louis was 99 percent black but if you were a white boy who managed to make it from your car to the inside of one of the gin joints, the owners ensured that no one caused trouble because they wanted the business, white and black. This was a world of jazz and Negroes, and people dressed extravagantly, a world that I not only had never seen but had never even imagined. The music took me to places I'd never been. People in these loud smoky music places would stare at us young white men, wondering if we were there for trouble or music or pussy or what, and in return I was full of wonderment and terror. I loved it and I've never forgotten it. Without the alcohol I would never have been running with the crowd who went to those joints and, sober, I would never have gone in any case.

Young guys I worked with at the steel mill were crazy. Not dark and unfunny crazy like my mother, but eccentric, wild, do-anything, bust-a-gut laughing crazy. I worked with one guy who was the horniest individual I've ever met in my life. At my age back then, mostly what we guys talked about was pussy . . . but also cars and guns and work and fighting. But this guy, a married schoolteacher who worked in the mills during summers to supplement his income, *all* he talked about was sex. Who he was fucking in addition to his wife. Who he'd like to fuck. Who he thought he could fuck. The various kinds of pussy he'd fucked, including the rare snapping pussy, which I had never heard of. He said there was good pussy and better pussy but the only bad pussy was no pussy. He told me he had fucked a chicken.

Another guy I went drinking with, one who knew all the bars and jazz joints, picked me up on our day off and said he was returning a pistol to the guy he bought it from because the damn gun was broken, he couldn't load it. I said let me take a look. He was a city guy who lived in the same projects where my aunt lived. I was staying with her to save on commuting. These were poor-white projects where we ate government commodities, peanut butter in two-gallon cans with a few inches of oil floating on top and dried milk that, if not mixed properly, would conceal marble-sized bombs of powder that came apart in your mouth and throat, threatening to choke you. The old man called the kids who lived in these projects "ridge runners" in honor of their Appalachian roots.

There was nothing wrong with the gun; this guy just didn't know how to slip the cartridges into the magazine at an angle. I showed him how and then racked the slide to make sure everything worked and then reloaded the magazine for him. He was grateful and told me to sit tight, he was going to see if his wife was at her sister's like she had said. "I told her I got called in to work today," he explained. "And she said she was going to her sister's. But if she ain't there, if she's with this guy I think she's with, then I'm going to shoot her."

He said this so flatly and conversationally that I wasn't sure I caught it right. "Shoot her?" I asked.

"Yep."

I didn't try to talk him out of it, even though I had uneasy thoughts of my prints being all over that pistol and magazine and cartridges. I did ask him if he was going to kill the guy, too. He said no, then explained his philosophy on this matter. "A guy will fuck any woman who lets him fuck her. I can't tell you how many of my buddies' wives I've fucked. And my wives' friends. In fact, this sister she's supposed to be visiting, I fucked her, too. It's up to the woman to say no. And if my wife ain't saying no to this guy, I'm going to shoot her. The guy, I'll just mess him up 'cause of the disrespect he's showing me by fucking my wife, take him out and whup his ass. But I won't shoot him."

On the ride to the wife's sister's house, my friend talked himself into actually doing it, progressing from the idea or possibility to the certainty of it—telling me he was intending at first just to shoot her in the leg or arm, but now he was going to put a fucking bullet right between her eyes. "They don't send you to the chair if you catch your wife with someone and then shoot either one of them. Couple years in the pen." The prospect was thrilling, being along when someone was on his way to murder someone—not terrifying as it had been when my father was intent upon killing my mother.

The wife was visiting with her sister just as she had told my friend, so nobody got shot that day. After he left them, on our way to a bar, he wondered aloud how much trouble he'd get in if he broached the subject of going to bed with his wife and sister at the same time. Once again, I had never heard of such a thing. "I'm pretty sure the sister would be up for it," he said. "And her husband's on afternoons, so we could bring our kids over to her house, get all the kids to bed, the three of us fuck, and then wake up our kids and get them back home before he gets off work. But you gotta be careful." I thought he was going to say careful about the husband coming home instead of being at work exactly as my friend had just done, trying to catch his wife cheating on him—but that's not what he was worried about. "If you throw out an idea like that, fucking your wife and her sister at the same time, and if she don't go for it, Jesus Christ, you'll never hear the end of it. And if you make the mistake of saying you think the sister will go for it, your wife will want to know why you think that, and then she'll figure out you're fucking her sister, and then the whole family will be pissed at you for, like, *years* to come."

So if my writing is violent and dark and profane and adolescently male—then consider the source, a life lived among working men who talked constantly of pussy and blood revenge . . . and a life lived on an isolated farm with crazy, violent people . . . and in poor people's project housing . . . and in house trailers . . . and with men who put firearms in their pockets before setting off to find out who their wives are with.

Alcohol also taught me where to find the hours I would need to write. Drinking and clubbing all night and then working at the steel mills launched a lifelong habit of going without sleep to get my work done. If I had not lived so crazily and had instead become one of those people who can't function without eight hours of sleep, then I would've never published thirteen books because most of them were written deep into the night when I had a regular day job and a family and stole my writing hours from my sleeping time.

I stopped drinking beer after I got out of the Air Force, because it was giving me ferocious headaches. I think I had gone through my lifetime allotment of beer. But I drank bourbon for a while and still had the headaches. Then at some point I had a gin and tonic and never looked back. I could drink gin all night long, and while it made me crazy *in* the head, it didn't hurt my head. Tanqueray and tonic when I could afford it. I've probably had ten thousand of them.

The first serious writing job I had was with an education magazine run by Jim Betchkal. The first day on the job he took me out to lunch at an ice cream shop in Evanston, Illinois. We had soup and a sandwich and, for dessert, a scoop of ice cream. As we were eating the ice cream on the way back to the office, Jim said, "Not all our lunches together are going to be this wholesome." It turned out to be one of the most profound understatements I've ever heard in my life.

Jim was a functioning alcoholic. He would come in very early every morning and work like a maniac. A brilliant editor, he taught me to love and respect words. He taught me grammar and syntax and subtlety. These lessons always came before lunch, however, because on most days he started drinking heavily at lunch, sometimes returning to the office to terrorize people, but often continuing the lunchtime drinking all afternoon until it was time to go home. He drank too much for any one of us to keep up with him, so he rotated his lunch partners, settling most often on me because he thought I had the most promise . . . as a writer and as a drunk.

He was savage in his criticisms and ridicule of my writing mistakes, but he also told me that I was a better natural writer than he'd ever been or ever would be. He said he knew *about* writing and could recognize good writing but was overly aware of his own writing's shortcomings, overly self-conscious, and could therefore never write as naturally and beautifully as I could. Part of my talent, he said, was in being so fucking ignorant about writing and writers that I wasn't even aware when something of mine was derivative, for example, and therefore I just allowed it to stand on its own. He said he would educate me about writers and writing without letting me lose my natural talent or become self-conscious about it. What he taught me altered my life. And it was all done in a constant soaking of alcohol. If I had not been his drinking companion, I would not have been his anointed.

Gin gave me the courage to risk something large for something good. I've always been ruthless about taking that risk—quitting great jobs whenever I had accumulated a little money ahead so I could write full time. And then when I ran out of money I went back to working full time until I was in a financial position to quit again. An accountant told me once that if I continued working and put all my book income into investments instead of quitting work and living on the book money as long as it lasted, I would be a multimillionaire. But you know what I wouldn't be, I told him—I wouldn't be a writer. This made no sense to him. It didn't make sense to my first wife, either.

Gin put me into bed with beautiful and crazy women I would've never had the nerve to talk with otherwise. Especially the crazy ones. A noncrazy friend of mine, Laura Lucs, told me a relationship theory that goes like this: You sometimes choose for a mate or companion a person who exhibits the negative behaviors that had an impact on you when you were powerless as a child. So a woman whose father withheld affection will choose a husband who is similarly cold. I'd heard this, of course, and had assumed the phenomenon arose from some perverse aspect of human nature that leads us to choose what we're familiar with even if it's destructive to us. But the theory my friend told me put a much more optimistic twist on it—that as adults we want to *fix* the behavior that we were powerless to fix as children. We therefore choose someone with the same problems so that *now*, as adults, we can make it better. According to this theory, I always chose crazy women not because I wanted to continue the problems I had with a crazy mother, but because I wanted the opportunity to remedy what I was unable to remedy as a child. I'm not sure if I believe this, but it's an optimistic twist on what would otherwise be interpreted as perverse and self-destructive behavior.

I was sitting in a bar once reading a book of Rimbaud's poetry. On the left-hand pages, the poems had been printed in French. On the right-hand pages were the English translations. A woman sits next to me. "You read French?" she asked. As I covered the right-hand page with my hand, I told her, "I would not insult Rimbaud by reading his poetry in any language other than the one he wrote in." We started going out together. She was crazy. She called my house and hung up when my wife answered, but if she got me she would insist on talking right then and there with my family about me. One time we were out drinking and she jumped on a table and started dancing, and her hair got caught in the overhead paddle fan, and we had to grab her and shout for someone to stop the fan, as I worried she might be snatched bald. At intimate moments, she asked me to say things in French. I made up French-sounding phrases and then translated them into my own poetry. All this was a gift from gin because I would never have had the wherewithal to act like such an asshole stone sober.

A friend familiar with my pattern said I could enter a room full of women and one might be bright and cheery and say she enjoys healthy sex, without recriminations . . . and another might be all smiles and say she would be supportive of her mate and she always looks on the bright side of life . . . and another might say she had a happy childhood and all of her adult relationships have been successful . . . and I'll meet them and smile and nod, but not be interested until I reach the woman in the corner, tears in her eyes, clothes dark and eccentric, a book of Rimbaud under the forearm that she is quietly stabbing with a pencil . . . and I'm, like, *helloooo, baby.*

I had an affair with a woman who, after a telephone call from me that didn't go her way, was crazy enough to get on an airplane in California and fly to Washington, D.C., where she marched into the company where I worked and raised hell with the CEO about my behavior and trashed my office (and later sent a letter to our board of directors). Then, before departing for California, she took a cab to my house, where she left some treasures that included letters I had written her and the panties she had apparently removed as she stood at our door while the cab waited in the street. My wife found everything. That was a disruption from which my first marriage never recovered.

Women are meaner than men when they're mad at you but more likely to forgive you in time. They have generous souls and are soft in many places. I love their logic. I love that you can talk them into things. When a woman in a bra leans just the right way, the bra strap pulls taut from the top of her shoulder to where the strap attaches to the top of the bra cup—and that suspension-bridge tension and the distance between the strap and her skin make for a scene more utterly fetching than anything I've ever written. I love watching a woman get dressed, the mysterious tucking and cinching, leaning and hooking, bringing everything together to a satisfying completion. A man just puts on clothes—a woman dresses as a performance. Not all of my adventures with women came about because of gin, but gin allowed me to be bold. And as William said, faint heart never won fair lady.

After a hard and concentrated day of writing, gin also quieted the crazy Guys in the Back Row so that they would finally leave me alone. I've been ruthless about how I use the Guys in the Back Row. During my writing hours, I call on them to help me imagine characters and remember things in my own life that inform the lives of my fictional characters. I make the Guys in the Back Row dance like monkeys for me, and I would never have become the writer I am today—good or bad—without the assistance of all that emotion I had on tap in the back row of my mind. But then when the writing was over, I needed the guys to give me some peace. I could not have functioned day to day if that emotion had continued after I stopped writing. That was my mother's condition—the madness, fears, and unholy emotions in her back row refused to shut up and leave her alone. The Guys in her Back Row were too strong—she would've had to stay drunk all the time to quiet them. When I went crazy in Tennessee, I stopped drinking gin and my guys took over and it was ugly.

After Norman Mailer died last fall, I read a story about him that talked of his early promise, saying that as a boy he had convinced his parents he was a genius and that his mother always knew he was destined for greatness. I thought at the time, how much *easier* the course must be if you start out with that kind of confidence and support. I didn't have either. Gin gave me both.

I wish I had drunk even more and reaped even more of the benefits in spite of gin's downsides, which have been precipitous.

A lot of the beautiful crazy women I had sex with, I had sex with while I was married the first time. I was a bad husband for eighteen years. Then I remarried and was a good husband for eighteen years. Yet both marriages ended in tears, at least partly because of gin. As someone who believes deeply and sincerely in honor, in doing the right thing, my record of cheating is shameful to me. If I wanted to have sex with beautiful crazy women, I should've divorced my wife and pursued the women openly instead of sneaking around like a creep. I hurt a lot of those beautiful crazy women by cheating on them with other beautiful crazy women. I have so little machismo left in me that you have to believe it when I say that none of this gives me any perverse pride for being a Great Lover. I wasn't. And the number of women isn't that high, but the intensity of the affairs was often devastating to everyone involved.

More than one person has pointed out to me the poetic justice or at least the goes-around-comes-around *aspect* of my life—that I collapsed in a shambles as a result of infidelity, whereas twenty years earlier, I had created so much shambles in so many lives as a result of *my* infidelity. I thanked the individuals who pointed this out to me, all of them women with whom I had affairs—but I really didn't need their insights in this particular case, because all along I have been painfully aware of circles being completed.

I was often bad while drinking gin. This was not a case of a good person doing bad things; I was a bad person. I embarrassed people and I embarrassed myself. Behavior that I thought cool was in fact as uncool as behavior can get. David Rosenthal, the Simon & Schuster editor I worked with for many years, once organized a book dinner that I showed up late for, after many of the editors and reviewers I was supposed to meet had left. Rosenthal was a gentleman and never said a word, but what the fuck was I thinking, drinking Tanqueray in a hotel room while he was embarrassed in front of those he had cajoled into coming to dinner for some writer they had never heard of, a writer who had so little respect for them and himself that he showed up late?

I missed out on the good parts of life because of the gin. I put people off. I got my ass kicked. I experienced years of severe lasting blackouts during which my behavior was so outrageous that I stopped asking people what I did last night and, instead, pleaded with them *not* to give me an account of what I said, what I did, who punched me, who I punched, when I got thrown out, and what I did and said as I was getting thrown out. I remember once—and one example will have to suffice—coming out of a blackout to find myself in an elevator in the middle of the day with businesspeople and I'm in a business suit, except that I am barefoot and I cannot remember where I am, where I am going, who I was with, under whose bed I left my shoes and socks, and what drama had been so urgent that it required my exit barefoot. When you're in this condition, businesspeople look at you in the strangest way, with scorn and contempt. Just like Mom. And this was back in the day when three-martini lunches were commonplace and it wasn't all that unusual to see someone tipsy in the afternoon—but not blackout-drunk and shoeless.

Another huge negative to alcohol was that while it initially had a calming effect on the Crazy Guys in the Back Row, dosage was critical. If I drank long enough and hard enough, the Crazy Guys came out of their stupor and went bat-shit.

When I was an executive with a national association, we held a conference in Miami. The plan was, I would go down for the business portion of the conference and then my first wife would join me after a few days so we could vacation. I agreed to bring her suitcase down with me so she could travel light when she came a few days later. After one of the business meetings, I got famously intoxicated and decided I would drive to Key West and look up a woman I had met during a writers' conference. Several rental cars had been assigned to our staff, but the car attendants wouldn't give me the keys because of my condition. I cornered one of the young men and took the keys from him, got in the car, sped away. I assumed the attendant would call the police, so I decided I'd better haul ass. It was after midnight when I got on Highway 1 and drove those one hundred and fifty miles to Key

West just as fast as I could go. At one point I was driving over a hundred miles an hour and I blasted through red lights. I guess I was trying to find out how far and how fast I would have to go before I got killed or stopped or shot. Amazingly, I made it all the way to Key West without incident. And then, even more amazingly, I managed to find the woman and get her on the phone and convince her to drive back to Miami with me. We arrived in my hotel room at dawn. She had recently broken her left arm and in moments of ecstasy kept hitting me on the side of the head with her plaster cast. When we finished and I was more or less sober, I began scrambling. First I had to get down to the morning meeting I was supposed to be chairing and make excuses, get someone to take my place; then I had to get *her* back to Key West. When I returned to the room, she wanted to know why there were women's clothes in my hotel room closet—the clothes I had hung up from the suitcase I had brought down for my wife. I said let's not worry about that, let's worry about getting you home. I'll buy you a plane ticket. And cab money to the airport. But she wouldn't take *cash* from me, what did I think she was, a prostitute? So we went to the airport together and I bought the ticket and handed her the ticket instead of the cash. Years later, when I was married to my second wife, this woman from Key West traveled to West Virginia and tried to look me up. She couldn't locate our farm. She did, however, take pictures of our local town and mail them to me to show how close she'd come.

I supposed it was only a matter of time until these gin adventures ended badly.

It finally happened after I'd been drinking all day and all night. One girlfriend wouldn't see me, another girlfriend wouldn't see me, and a third girlfriend agreed to see me but then wouldn't have anything to do with me because I was such a mess. I desperately did not want to go home and face my wife's wrath for having been gone all night, so I got on my motorcycle and decided to drive home to Illinois, a thousand miles away. At the time, we were living outside Washington, D.C. I blacked out at some point and woke up—that is, my memory resumed—to find myself on an interstate at 3 a.m. in a driving rainstorm. I was soaked and sick. Drunk but no longer drunk enough to be oblivious of the danger I was in. Huge eighteen-wheelers blew their air horns at me as a signal to get off the freaking highway. I don't know what kept the motorcycle from going over as those big trucks went by and sprayed me. I finally took an exit, pulled into the first motel I came to, and pressed the buzzer until someone showed up to rent me a room. As I was filling out the paperwork, the old guy stared at me and finally said, "You should've stopped before this." I thought he was referring to how wet I was until I got to the room and looked in the mirror.

In that cheap motel room (how many terrible adventures have started with those words?), I had an attack of anxiety worse than anything I had suffered before. I had vivid hallucinations, specifically of blob creatures crawling on the wall and around the radiator. I talked—babbled—to myself constantly. Some of these symptoms are earmarks of delirium tremens, the pink elephant DTs, but DTs are the result of withdrawal from alcohol, and I was still on a binge. I did not change out of my wet clothes or shower or try to sleep. The anxiety was too terrifyingly acute for me to do anything but sit on the bed hugging myself and wishing for morning.

Dawn brought light, but not sanity or hope. I found a phone book and began checking for nearby mental hospitals. I found one fairly close. I got a recording, this being dawn, so I called back every few minutes until I spoke with someone, got directions, and rode there on my motorcycle. I thought that by the time I arrived, with the rain and night over, I'd feel better, and maybe a hearty breakfast would put me right and I could forget about checking myself in. But the hallucinations and anxiety didn't stop, I couldn't eat, and I showed up at the hospital asking for help.

(Again, the parallels with my early life, with my mother, with my father are vivid. We took my mother to an asylum without notice or appointment, just the way I was showing up at this mental institution. Sometimes life feels less like a journey than a ride on a merry-go-round.)

The hospital wasn't in a hurry to admit me. I hadn't been referred by anyone, had come in off the streets. After a couple of hours, I was taken to see an admitting psychiatrist, who asked me the usual questions and then wanted to know, specifically, why I had come to the hospital. I told him I saw things happening in my peripheral vision. I said that pencil there on his desk had started moving like an inchworm but when I looked at it, it stopped. I said I see something tumbling down that hill outside his window. In fact, my tendency to see things move in my peripheral vision occurs even today . . . a holdover or reminder from the days when I was crazy, except now the phenomenon is not that severe and I've accommodated it, as I have the various obsessive-compulsive routines I feel compelled to perform so that I and members of my family come to no harm.

The psychiatrist said he was admitting me of my own volition, which meant I could check myself back out. I liked that part. First I would have to have a complete physical by the facility's regular medical doctor. Damnedest thing, that. I was taken to a subbasement, into a windowless room, and I had the strangest feeling that it was the facility's morgue—although why a mental hospital would have a morgue, I don't know. But it had that cold isolation feel of a morgue. I was a corpsman in the Air Force, I know what a morgue feels like.

I waited near an examining table. In comes Dr. Strangelove, tall, thick features, horn-rim glasses. He had me strip naked and lie down. He seemed jolly, amused by the proceedings. This very strange doctor in a central casting white smock did the usual examination of thumping and feeling and listening with his stethoscope. While I lay buck naked on the examining table. And then the son of a bitch commented on my dick. "I bet the girls like that, huh?"

You don't have to be crazy to work there, but I suppose it helps.

An attendant took me to a small room. Bed, table, empty bookshelf, and small bathroom with a toilet and sink, but no tub or shower. A nurse came in and took all my possessions, including my belt and the shoelaces from my rain-ruined shoes before shutting and *locking* the heavy door behind her. When I was brought supper that evening, I mentioned the locked door and reminded the attendant that I had checked in voluntarily and could therefore leave any time I wanted to. I said this rather haughtily, as if reminding a flight attendant of my first-class status. She looked at me with pity for my ignorance. "Checking yourself out," she informed me, "requires a certain *procedure*. It's not a matter of walking out. We can't have our patients just walk away any time they feel like it." And with that, she left and shut *and locked* the door once again.

On my dinner tray the nurse had left one of those little paper cups, like the kind you put ketchup in at a fast-food restaurant, containing my pills. She told me I should take them with my meal, but she didn't actually wait and watch me take them. I don't know if this was an oversight on her part or was procedure for voluntary patients, allowing them to take or not take their medications as they chose. I flushed them down the toilet. I've had prescriptions for (or have been advised to take) various psychotropic medicines or antidepressants at various junctures in my life but have always refused on the theory that what's going on in my mind is what I write about, and if I mess with what the Guys in the Back Row are saying, what they're weeping and wailing about, then I've messed with the material that underlies my writing. A doctor once told me that of all the reasons he's ever heard for people not taking antidepressants, mine was the stupidest.

The voice from a patient in a room across the hall from mine sounded like it belonged to a teenage boy. He cursed the nurses with an inventive eloquence—magnificent profanity that he took his time with and articulated with exquisite precision, his curses beautiful in their anguish.

I checked myself out the next day, my wife came to fetch me home, and I attended a few mandatory sessions with a shrink. I stopped drinking for a while but my sober life was boring. Without alcohol I had no way to quiet the Guys in the Back Row, no way to fuel adventures that I was too timid to undertake sober. I eventually returned to gin, which took me back with juniper kisses.

The bad parts of alcohol that I regret most involve the time I lost with my sons when they were growing up. During my awful night in Tennessee when I came within a few trigger-pull pounds of killing myself, what cringed my soul most was being a bad father. Today I am close to my sons. I enjoy their company more than I do that of any other individuals on earth. This is joy. To witness Matthew David Martin and Joshua Robert Martin turning out to be successful and honorable men. To admire their wives, Amanda and Kathy. To adore my granddaughter, Pearl Lucille, and my grandson, Samuel Lucius. And I am aware, fully, of how unearned this joy is and at what risk I put it years ago by drinking so much.

And now? No. Maybe the Guys in the Back Row have simply grown weary of screaming, of crying, of remembering. And now, too tired, they don't need to be either kept in line or liberated with gin. Does it sound like I'm going gently into that good night? I would prefer to believe that my current state has been granted to me not through surrender but through the grace of time and survival.

8

AN UNFORTUNATE MARRIAGE

I BEGAN DATING my first wife when we were in high school. We went to different colleges but still dated more or less exclusively during those years, and after I got out of the Air Force we were married and had kids right away. We were twenty-six when our second son was born. I think being together since we were fourteen gave us such a sense of inevitability that neither of us felt a pressing need to maintain what we assumed was everlasting. It was, unfortunately, an unhappy marriage from the very beginning, although I would never regret a marriage that produced two sons such as ours. My wife and I argued about everything. We were so miserable together that I tried to spend as much time away from her as I possibly could. I drank heavily and regularly and the alcohol lubricated my way toward multiple infidelities. I was uninterested in the suburban family activities she loved. I spent every waking sober hour at the typewriter.

As I pursued magazine jobs, we lived in Chicago; in Evanston, Illinois; outside of San Francisco; and then in Washington, D.C. Throughout these years, I kept writing, kept sending off stories, desperate to get published. Seeing my self-imposed deadline of having a book published by the time I was thirty come and go, I became all the unhappier, drinking even more, engaging in crazy affairs. In the late 1970s, a short story of mine was a finalist in a magazine contest, and one of the judges sent the story to Marian Wood of Holt, Rinehart & Winston. Marian called me, said she liked the story, and asked if I was working on a book. This was the dream call I'd been waiting for my entire adult life. I was in fact working on a book, which Holt published in 1979—my first novel, *Tethered*.

My second novel, *The Crying Heart Tattoo,* came out in 1982 to great reviews (a *New York Times* Notable Book of the Year), strong sales to foreign publishers, and promising movie interest.

I had been so reverential about writing that, before my books were published, I never told people I was a writer. If someone asked what I did, I said I was a magazine editor, said I worked at such-and-such foundation or association. I didn't feel like a legitimate writer until I was published. Which finally happened when I was thirty-three. Thank God and Marian Wood.

But being a real writer didn't make the marriage any happier. In reaction to my wife's complaints about me, I withdrew into sullen silence, which made her all the angrier that I wouldn't talk things out, wouldn't open up. Miserable in her presence, I was a profound disappointment to her and her family.

I quit a regular job for a while and wrote full time, but the money ran out and I went back to work. Except for that year I took off to write full time, I had high-level jobs during the entire eighteen-year marriage. I wrote fiction at night after my sons and wife went to bed, writing sometimes until three or four in the morning and then getting a few hours of sleep before going to my job. On occasion I would write all night. If my son, Josh, got up in the morning and found me still at my desk, he would tell his mother a slogan he had heard stores use, that Dad "was open twenty-four hours a day." After those all-night sessions, I would be so exhausted when I came home from work that I could call my other son, Matt, to time me falling asleep. I'd hand him my wristwatch, ask him to keep track of the second hand, and remember to tell me later how long it took me to fall asleep on the floor. Twenty seconds, forty seconds, never more than one minute. I lived in a state of constant exhaustion.

And then all bets—and vows and promises and devotion to my sons—were off when I fell crazy in love with another woman and my marriage ended as it had proceeded for eighteen years: bitterly.

9

A BEAUTIFUL MARRIAGE

S HE PRECEDED me down a spiral staircase the day I met her and as we spiraled around, taking the steps quickly, there was about her a certain *bounce* that restored hope. She would come into a room, her smile up around a thousand watts, and I'd be sitting there in my miserable writerly mood, drawing on the unfiltered Camel and wincing at her good cheer as I said to her, "What is this happy horseshit?"

Whatever it was—brightness and optimism and a undaunted life force—it was powerful enough to make *me*, the world's most miserable man, happy.

More than once we went into a restaurant, ordered lovely meals, and then an hour later the waiter took the food away, untouched. Because we talked. She loved books and read constantly. Our affair was crazy and her mother told her that it would come to no good; he's married with two kids and you're just a piece of ass to him. But I was mad for her and realized for the first time in my life what a soul mate meant. Two decades later I would come to appreciate the downside to having a soul mate—that when you lose her, you lose everything.

We loved each other's company, we never argued, were best friends, could sit and talk for hours. We were never sappy or clingy, at least not in public, but we were one of those couples about whom other people say, I hope someday I can have a marriage like theirs. As rapidly as I could, I separated from my wife, filed for divorce, and when the divorce was final, this new woman and I moved to the farm, neither of us with gainful employment. I was paying alimony and child support. Battles with my ex-wife were ongoing. Still, these were the best years of my life because this woman and I were crazy in love.

We wanted to live on a farm. She wanted animals. I wanted to be in the country even though when I left home at eighteen I had declared I would never live on a farm again. This was going to be different. This was not the old man's farm, this would be my farm. And hers. Ours.

We looked at a dozen different places in Virginia and West Virginia. I wanted to be close enough that I could get to my sons within a day's drive. They were teenagers and didn't want much to do with me. I had handled the divorce and remarriage as clumsily as anyone ever had, but I still needed to know I wasn't more than a few hours away from them.

Farms we liked we couldn't afford. Farms we could afford we didn't like. We'd been squired around by a number of good ol' boy rednecks in the real estate business, but the man showing us a farm outside of Alderson, West Virginia, was the owner. We met somewhere in town and he picked us up in his rattling old truck. He had on dirty jeans and a work shirt. I spoke slowly to make sure he could understand a city slicker like me. "What line of work are you in?" I asked.

He smiled. "I'm an orthopedic surgeon and in my free time I carve violins."

Oh.

The woman and I (we were not yet married) had discussed a real estate plan of action. If we saw a property we liked, we would play it cool. Never show our interest. Perhaps even gently point out the property's shortcomings.

When the doctor turned into the lane and we saw the farm for the first time, my crazy love started hollering, "It's perfect! It's what we've been looking for! I can't believe it, this is *exactly* what I had in mind."

It didn't matter that he knew we loved the place because we could afford only a certain amount of money, and this farm was right at that mark.

And what we got for our $89,000 was a house with two or three electrical outlets and no central heat. We warmed ourselves with woodstoves that we had no idea how to operate that first winter. A glass of water on the nightstand would be frozen by morning. I couldn't start writing until the house warmed up enough that my IBM Selectric typewriter would work. I think the machine's lubrication froze or congealed overnight, paralyzing operations until the temperature in the house climbed above 50.

The old house's two screw-in fuses were in a box attached to the side of the house, *outside*, so that when you went out at night to replace a fuse, a frequent occurrence because two appliances going at once would blow a fuse, you'd be standing there in the dew-wet grass or maybe in a driving rain, hoping against hope against electrocution.

For most of our years on the farm, we didn't have television. At night we talked and read. We raised German shepherds from Tanqueray, our male, and Jamaica, our female.

We were fine as long as we were poor. When my thrillers began earning significant money, we upped our spending (on horses, trucks, trailers, tractors—a farm offers nearly endless opportunities for spending, a lesson I obviously did not learn from my childhood). Then we made the mistake from which we never recovered: when the successful years came to a close, we didn't have the sense or courage to live poor again.

10

BEING DUMB ABOUT MONEY

As you read over the next few pages on how I fucked up my financial life, there's no judgment or condemnation you can level against me that's any harsher than those I've already delivered against myself. I have spent the five years I've been recovering from losing everything trying to figure out why it happened. I've come to realize that a portion of the financial collapse must have been willful. I come from the working poor, welfare poor, trailer poor. I've been a steel mill union member, a proletariat who mistrusts the rich, so I suppose one explanation for my self-destructive behavior was that I was ashamed of having money and became unconsciously determined not to have any anymore. In this, I was enormously successful.

I agree with the belief that if you don't love money, money won't love you. I believe that people who care about money and think about money and are lovingly careful with money have a greater chance of being rewarded by getting and keeping money.

Neither my wife nor I cared about money. We showed our contempt for money by spending it. By spending money, you are getting rid of it, rejecting it, showing your desire to be free of it. For years on end, we were hateful like that toward money—and money eventually left us for good.

My first four books were well-received literary novels, but I began to write thrillers that began to sell . . . movie options, paperback, foreign sales. My income inched up year by year until income from the books was approaching half a million dollars a year. My wife eventually had upwards of twenty horses. I had two trucks, two cars. We bought houses in town where I could get away from the farm and write. We traveled. We bought more land.

My agent at the time, Bob Dattila, told me I should be saving more to prepare for the hard times that would inevitably come. I listened but didn't follow his advice. I wrote thrillers for money. Every time I thought we were heading for financial trouble, another $200,000 book deal or $100,000 movie option was signed. Only later did I arrive at the truth that you can never earn your way out of financial problems; you must underspend your way out. Think of rock stars or boxing champs, making multiple millions of dollars and still going bankrupt.

We had years of warning as the literary gravy train slowed. But even when the train stopped completely, my wife and I stayed onboard, buying things through open windows.

When we were still living on the farm, we'd lie in bed before going to sleep and talk about money. "You have to get rid of some horses," I'd tell her.

She'd agree—and then mention a couple of mares that were pregnant and how, after they have their foals, or when the foals are weaned, she could sell both the mothers and the offspring.

"But if your horses are having babies, the herd is getting *bigger,* not smaller."

"I know," she said. "But it doesn't make sense to sell the mares while they're pregnant. If we wait until the babies are on the ground— or even better, weaned—we'll have more animals to sell, make more money. Don't worry, eventually I'll sell enough to get down to two or three."

I said, "I guess I shouldn't have bought that brand-new tractor."

"No," she told me, "we needed it. The old tractor was a mess, and what's the point of living on a farm if you can't raise animals and work the farm with a tractor?"

"You're right. If we don't have animals and equipment, we might as well move to town."

And thus we enabled each other as if we were addicts, telling each other that we're going to quit soon, that we can handle it, that the addictions are not an insurmountable problem, not yet, not for us. Talking about our financial problems and coming up with future plans for dealing with those problems seemed to count, in our minds, as actually *doing* something. Meanwhile the financial slide continued, horse by horse, tool by tool.

The fact we got along so well and never argued eventually worked against us, because I never said no to buying another horse and she never said no to me about a piece of equipment or a writing trip.

We were together eighteen years. For the first nine, my income got higher and higher each year. Then for the second nine, it declined year by year.

I didn't love money enough, so money left me. I didn't pay enough attention to my writing career, so it too abandoned me. I thought my job was to write the books, my agent's job was to make deals with publishers, and my publishers' job was to sell the books. But I was wrong. It was my career, and if I wasn't responsible for it, who was?

When I talk with other people about losing everything, one theme comes up time after time: They felt stupid. They felt worthless. Their decisions and actions left them with a gnawing self-loathing. How could I have been so dumb? they ask themselves—dumb about a marriage or a business partnership. That's how I feel when I think of all the money we went through and how self-destructive we were about not saving any of it.

In yet another example of life repeating itself, I realize now that I did what my father did: lost money on a farm. My parents argued about money for years, and even as a child, I knew that the root cause of their money problems was the farm. Yet, as my income got lower and lower, we kept spending $10,000 a month on horses and tractors and building barns and other farm projects that never returned a cent of profit.

My wife continued to talk of how she was going to sell some of her horses but, instead of selling them, she bought more. I would order tools and equipment that I was convinced I needed to operate the farm but then never got around to taking the stuff out of the boxes. Tragically, we ended up selling everything—horses recently purchased and tools still brand-new in their boxes—for pennies on the dollar.

She was the one who finally suggested cutting the Gordian knot. I had been spending more time away from the farm, living awhile in New Orleans to write my book, *Pelikan*. One morning she walked into the old Victorian house we had bought in town, a house I used as my writing office and where I was plotting another extended writing trip. She said, "We should sell the farm."

"Sell Blue Goose?"

"Yes," she said. I think she wanted me to talk her out of it. She has regretted until this very day that we sold the farm.

I asked, "Are you sure?"

She said, "You want to, don't you?" Testing me. I was supposed to say, We'll never sell Blue Goose. We'll find a way to make it work. But instead I said yes. I said I wanted to get out from under the money we were spending, so yes, let's do it. It was like deciding to rob a bank. Surely this was not something we were serious about. One of us will say, Hey, this is ridiculous, we're not going to do this. But neither of us tried to talk the other out of it.

And that's how the decision was made. It was perverse, as if we were daring each other, each of us waiting for the other to call the bluff. *Of course we're not going to sell the farm, I just wanted to see what you'd say.* But the dare went forward. She was tired of me complaining about how much money we were spending on the farm, and I couldn't figure out how to make us stop the spending.

Our friends and my family were appalled. How can you sell a place you love so much and have worked on so hard? We didn't tell people the truth—that we didn't have the wherewithal to stop ourselves from spending $10,000 a month with an income of half that. So we closed our eyes and sold Blue Goose and all of our equipment, the cars and trucks and our extra land and all the horses and our house in town, in auctions that lasted an entire weekend.

Because we had bought the farm for so little and had built it into a showplace and had so much *stuff* to sell, the auctions repaid our debts and replenished our bank accounts. But this financial healing cost us the magic that once defined our lives.

Debt-free, with serious money in the bank, we now had a second chance. We could've moved to the city, both gotten jobs, built a solid financial foundation, and then maybe in five years or so we could have moved back to the country with enough money to live a happy, modest life until the end.

But instead I insisted I already had a full-time job—writing—and my wife insisted that whatever little money she could make wouldn't support our lifestyle, so what was the point?

Where were we going to move? I wanted something that was the opposite of a farm. New York City? No, after having given up so much, she couldn't live in the city and she wouldn't give up her dog. I got it in my head that southwest Florida, some boating community, would be the perfect anecdote to farm life.

I said, "We'll move to Florida and get a boat. We'll fish among the islands. Cook the day's catch on a deserted beach and spend the night at anchor. Have just one dog instead of all the horses, cows, dogs, cats we had on the farm. What do you think?"

She said okay. No enthusiasm, no criticism, no alternative suggestions. My wife was in shock from having sold the place she loved most in the world, and she dealt with that shock by clamming up and going along with whatever I suggested. Instead of being the bright-wattage optimist of our lives, she became as withdrawn as a novelist.

We hated Florida. After working hard every day on the farm, we were appalled by the leisure-centric lifestyle. We hated that there were no woods to walk through. We hated that dogs were unwelcome in so many places. Unfortunately, we hated it *after* we bought land on which to build a dream house and *after* purchasing a condo to live in while the dream house was being built. As soon as those purchases were made, my wife went into a severe funk. She'd been the most active person I'd ever known, but now she just sat and stared. If you've ever made a major, life-changing, and expensive decision and then realized almost immediately that it was wrong on all counts, you know how the regret can hollow you out. We'd get up in the middle of the night, neither of us able to sleep, and drive the empty highways, through the Everglades on Alligator Alley. We were stopped once by a state cop, not for speeding but just for being out and about in the Everglades at 3 a.m. "Where you heading?" he wanted to know. "Just driving," I told him. "We couldn't sleep so we're just driving around." He didn't believe me, but he couldn't find anything wrong and let us go.

When my wife decided she couldn't tolerate Florida a moment longer, she left with our dog to go live with her sister in Virginia while I tried to sell the land and the condo that we had purchased just weeks before.

We held Florida in such small regard that we didn't even decorate the condo, which was a model with its own furniture and art and a cardboard television to show what a television would look like in the living room. As a final homey touch, the picture frames throughout the condo were fitted with photographs, cut from magazines, of smiling people.

I remember waking in the morning after my wife had gone north. I would turn toward the bedside table and see the picture frame holding the magazine photograph of a very happy blond woman. Why was I waking up next to her? It was awful. I drank a lot. The other condos were populated with retirees who plotted their days from golf course to cruise line to the evening's restaurant selection. Florida is the only place I've ever lived that I didn't incorporate in a book. I hated it. In an attempt to recoup some small portion of the happiness we lost with Blue Goose, we spent money on stupid things we couldn't afford, like a $60,000 RV, and we traveled and we chipped away at the money our farm had given us.

Still, I was always expecting that the next book, the next movie deal, would bail us out, as books and movies had always bailed us out before.

Finally, taking losses, we got out from under the land and condo.

If Florida was the opposite of West Virginia, the next place we moved, Saratoga Springs in upstate New York, was supposed to be the opposite of Florida. A nice book contract had finally come through and we still had money left from selling the farm. So God and grace and Blue Goose and Simon & Schuster had given us another chance. That would be our second chance to be smart about money. We still could've done what we should've done after selling the farm. We could've started a modest life in a modest house, with both of us working in modest jobs. Bank the money. Heal. But that's not the way we went.

As part of my unconscious but successfully ruinous effort to become poor again, I bought a beautiful antebellum mansion in Saratoga Springs, New York—seven thousand square feet with triple garage, twelve acres of grounds, swimming pool, big two-story columns in front of the house to establish a veranda. A guy came out to clean the pool and I asked him how much he thought it might cost to heat it. He looked at the towering house and the three-car garage and the manicured grounds—and he said, "What do you care what anything costs?" I was embarrassed. I wanted to say, No, wait, you don't understand, I'm a workingman like you. But of course I wasn't like him. I used to be like him and I was on my way to being like him again, but at the time I had enough money to live in a mansion.

I would walk the long, tree-lined lane from that house to get the mail. Across the way from the mailbox was a modest bungalow situated close to the road. One morning I saw a grizzled old guy out in the yard and waved to him. He replied, "Get a job, asshole." I guess the assumption was that I was one of the idle rich with nothing better to do than walk to the mailbox and collect my annuity checks. I wanted to tell him that I worked twelve hours a day, seven days a week, writing and writing and trying to keep this enterprise together.

But instead of explaining to people that I was not rich, I systematically endeavored to *become* poor.

After two years in Saratoga Springs, that last good book deal money had been spent and we had to sell out and move somewhere cheap. We didn't have another chance to be stupid about money because there was no money left about which to be stupid. We were finally successful in getting rid of the last of the money we didn't love.

Good friends of ours in Saratoga Springs, Larry and Geraldine Abrams, were real estate agents who sold our house and didn't take a commission—that's how generous-hearted they were and how financially desperate we were. A year ago Geraldine died of cancer. The day before her death, their son, Joshua, died of an accidental drug overdose. It makes me ashamed to call this book *Losing Everything*.

TENNESSEE, OUR BITTER END

BITTER END is a nautical term referring to the end of a rope or chain that's onboard a ship and often wrapped around a bitt or vertical post. The term, *bitter end,* refers not only to the *bitt end* of the rope but also to the unhappy consequence of allowing that end of the rope or chain to unwrap from the bitt and get pulled overboard, lost. You need to do something before that happens. Secure the rope. Stop the chain from running out or link it to another chain. Whatever you do, don't let matters go until you reach the bitter end.

Our being dead-broke after Saratoga Springs meant that our lifeline was unspooling, but I suppose we did have one final chance to secure the bitter end. With the last of our money we bought a little farm near Paris, Tennessee. It cost about a fourth of what the house in Saratoga Springs was worth. The Tennessee house was so small it might have fit in the garage of our house in Saratoga Springs. Now that we didn't have any money left, our last chance could have been starting from zero and slowly building our way back up. But we didn't. Instead we plunged all the more deeply into debt.

Someone asked if my wife and I talked about this financial freefall while it was happening.

We did, but in the wrong terms, not how could we stop the fall but when and by what means might we be rescued before hitting bottom. When were we going to get a movie deal? When would that magic front-page review of a book ignite a best seller? Like the losers at Harry Hope's saloon, we invested in our pipe dreams.

I noticed something else in Tennessee, our last stand, the bunker, our bitter end—it was no longer the two of us against the world. That alliance had apparently ended in Florida when she left me to go live with her sister—left me to my own mistake, I would say in her defense, because Florida was resolutely my idea. In Tennessee we were together day and night, but our spiritual separation continued. She'd always had her horses and I'd always had my writing, but in all other things we had always been a team. I was her biggest fan and she championed all my causes. Should anyone say anything against her, that person was my enemy—and she jumped to my defense if anyone criticized me. But in our Tennessee bunker, the iron team began to crack.

One afternoon she came back from visiting a woman friend, and when I asked why the woman had called her, my wife said the woman and her husband were having some troubles. What kind of troubles, I asked. She said she couldn't tell me, she didn't want to betray a confidence. This was the first time to my knowledge we had ever kept anything from each other and I mark it as a sign of the beginning of the end. Before, when she promised people who told her secrets that she wouldn't tell a soul, she used to add, "Except for David, because I tell David everything." No more.

I remember another incident that showed we were drifting. We were cutting brush that was threatening to short out our electric fence. On one steep section we walked single file, with my wife following me. We both carried machetes. "David?" she asked. "Yeah?" I replied and kept walking up the hill. She said, "I have an overwhelming desire to bury this machete in the back of your head." I stopped and looked at her and laughed. She didn't laugh back. I suggested maybe she wanted to walk ahead of me.

During flush times, our credit cards raised their credit limits until we had something like $80,000 credit on four cards. That's what we lived on. Run up one card to the maximum, then make the minimum payments each month with the help of the next card we were maxing out.

Seeking even more credit to help us go even more deeply into debt, I applied for a new credit card and was turned down. The process was completed electronically so I didn't suffer the embarrassment of having a *person* pass judgment on me by telling us we were way over our head in debt—but I was still shamed by the turndown.

During that year in my first marriage when I tried to make full-time writing work, our finances got so low that I went to the bank to deposit a check that our Visa card had sent us, drawn on our credit card. Back then, checks from credit card accounts were still somewhat unusual, so the teller called over a fuck-face bank manager. He looked at the check, looked at me, then asked the teller to call up my account. When he saw the amount, he shared a private laugh with the teller and said, in front of me, "No wonder he wants to cash a credit card check . . . he's got $1.36 in his account."

William Faulkner was postmaster at the University of Mississippi's post office for almost three years. He spent a lot of time in the back office working on his fiction rather than coming up front to sell folks their stamps. Finally a postal inspector convinced him to resign. Faulkner's comment: "I reckon I'll be at the beck and call of folks with money all my life, but thank God I won't ever again have to be at the beck and call of every son of a bitch who's got two cents to buy a stamp."

Bill and I have that in common—both of us at the beck and call of people with money.

My wife and I were in Tennessee a year, and our situation kept getting worse and worse, but then *magic*. It seemed we would be rescued after all. What we had so foolishly hoped for began at long last to happen: we were going to have a Big Book that got sold to the movies. In 2002, my novel, *Crazy Love,* was published to great reviews. An ecstatic one in the *Los Angeles Times* generated serious movie interest, including phone calls to my agent from representatives of A-list stars who wanted to buy or option the book. We sensed a big paycheck coming our way. Out of debt. Never in it again. My wife and I talked about how we were going to change our ways. I sensed that the old team, the two of us against the world, had a chance of reuniting.

In the middle of the *potential* of this deliverance, there was an argument among agents/producers/lawyers—and all the pending deals evaporated. People in Hollywood dread like death the threat of lawsuits, and as word of a potential lawsuit went out, the flurry of early interest in *Crazy Love* died away.

Still, I mistakenly thought the threatened lawsuit itself had nothing to do with me, sitting on our little farm in Tennessee, broke, while the wealthy of Hollywood argued. A Hollywood legal battle was preventing my book from becoming a movie when I needed that movie more than ever, but the lawsuit itself couldn't touch me because—ha-ha—I had no assets.

The laugh was on me. One of the people came after me personally. He called repeatedly and at first I was blasé. What could he do to me? I was broke. But then in one of the phone calls, this person informed me he would pursue something of value I still did own: the copyrights to my books, numbering ten at that time. After acquiring ownership of my copyrights in a lawsuit, this person informed me, he would sell them to various movie companies. Then movies would be made, except I would get nothing from the movies because I would no longer own my books.

I went on a search for a lawyer to represent me. None would. Even though I was convinced this Hollywood person had no case against me, the lawyers I talked with required retainers. I was broke.

Abandoning all pretense of writing, I devoted myself to the *Bleak House* of this threatened lawsuit. The Hollywood person kept calling, kept demanding, made calls to those I did business with, made demands, threatened further legal action.

As this continued for months, my wife and I approached the debt limits of our credit cards. She worked with her horses, went on trail rides, tried to make connections that might lead to sales of various horses, but she remained adamant about not getting an office job. I applied for work at a nearby factory. There it was. Started out life as the son and grandson and nephew of steel mill workers, began my work life in those mills, and now after college, after being a successful magazine editor, being the vice president of a national association, spending nearly twenty years as a full-time novelist—*now*, in my fifties, I was going to have to work in a factory again. I suspect that the Hollywood person who believed I was part of a conspiracy to do him wrong is deeply satisfied to know how low I had sunk.

A new wood products factory was opening locally and I went to fill out an application and take a battery of tests. As I waited among the working poor, some of them unemployed and others hoping for a better job, I think I felt that something had been made right with the world, though at a terrible cost. I didn't deserve success or money. Here's what I deserved, to be among the people I was born to. Working men and women. Why had I put on airs? Who the fuck did I think I was? A novelist? What an asshole. Welcome home, David.

But wait . . . there's more. Both of my parents were diabetics and I knew from my symptoms, which had shown up a year or so before, that I had the disease, too. I was consumed by a constant thirst as my body was trying to dilute and then excrete the excess glucose in my system. I was always hungry, craving sugar because the sugar in my system wasn't being metabolized but was floating around in my blood and urine, fucking up my capillaries. I pissed like a racehorse. I knew I had the disease but I couldn't bear going to a doctor to have it confirmed—there would be a regimen of treatment, of prescription drugs, and my wife and I had no insurance and no money to pay for drugs. Basically I couldn't afford to have the disease I so clearly had. I didn't know how high my glucose levels were, but they must've been off the charts, making me even crazier than I already was. I knew what this disease was doing to my health; I remember amputations being done on my father, my grandparents. The prospect of this disease and the need to do something about it continued to press heavily on me as the rest of my life continued spiraling out of control.

And at the absolute depth and maximum weight of these troubles, my wife began an affair with a man she went riding with. A married man. Had a kid. Came into my house as a friend. I served coffee to warm them up before they went on early morning rides, and later I heard him tell her that he had tried to befriend me in hopes that the friendship would throw me off the trail of what the two of them were doing.

My wife's affair might not have been sexually consummated until after I lost my mind and left Tennessee—so many lies had been planted in the maintenance of the affair that the actual truth was lost to me. It doesn't matter. I caught her talking to him in ways that made it clear they were intimate.

When I confronted her, she said she wanted to stay married to me and never see him again, so we started working on that. Then a few days later I caught her returning to him. She said she wanted to see him one last time to put an end to what was going on between them but she still passionately wanted our marriage to work. Okay, let's try again. We took walks and talked. Then I caught her going back to him a third time.

You will note the language I'm using to describe what was happening: I *caught her . . . confronted her . . . caught her a third time*. The lies and deceptions required by an affair fit precisely in the embrace of my paranoia and I danced like a madman for weeks while she kept promising not to call him, then called him.

Eventually, she and I had a night that was nearly as awful as the night when I was twelve and my father almost killed my mother. But for that second terrible night to occur, something more than her affair was needed.

Because even with all that was going on . . . the multiyear slide into publishing oblivion . . . the stupid financial decisions that led us so deeply into debt . . . the nagging threat of a lawsuit that promised to take away ownership of my books . . . the haunting knowledge that I had an untreated disease . . . the perceived betrayals of a soul mate . . . even with all of that, one other ingredient was needed to entice me to hold a revolver to my forehead and watch as the hammer pulled slowly back . . . to force me to shoot into the wall of our house to get her attention . . . to hear voices urging death all around . . . to buy large locks and secure myself in a spare bedroom each night out of fear that she was going to kill me . . . to be escorted out of a store babbling about plots against me . . . and to end up on the dining room floor, crawling on all fours, wailing as my head tossed from side to side like a gut-shot bear, curling into a fetal ball that wasn't nearly tight enough to offer protection from the beast ravishing me, having a phone held to my ear so I was forced to hear my son say the same three words over and over, repeating a hundred times the words that prevented me from blowing out my brains.

The extra special ingredient that supercharged all those other misfortunes was something I had pushed and pulled through life ever since its creation in a strange childhood: madness.

12

LIES AND MADNESS

FOR THE two years we were in Tennessee before I discovered her affair, I followed a bogus work pattern—rising in the late morning to brew a pot of coffee and reading a paper or magazine, going into my office to pretend to work for a few hours, then puttering around the farm. My ferocious capacity to work was no longer available to me. And the stuff I did write back then was facile and superficial and grasping toward some notion of notoriety or flash. No wonder she stopped respecting me. I had stopped respecting myself. I had stopped acting with dignity or honor. I took us deeper into debt to buy her things we couldn't afford and she hadn't asked for: a truck and a horse trailer and a remodeled barn and, of course, there was always another horse to buy. Maybe I was trying to buy (on credit card debt) the love that I could no longer earn on my own. Our once-intense sex life dwindled to pathetic fumblings.

My high point of each day was the first gin I drank as she made dinner. (Eventually, I wouldn't eat anything she prepared for fear she would poison me.) Then another one during dinner. Then another one afterward. Large, generous gins ever so light on the tonic . . . I wanted to be anesthetized. My life was a failure and I just wanted to stop being reminded of that, wanted it to stop hurting. After dinner, I usually fell asleep or passed out on the couch in front of the television, fat and snoring. I can't imagine what she found unattractive about me.

And then one day I picked up the phone and heard her talking to him. With madness hovering nearby, this was a conversation I did not need to have in my head.

Betrayal resides on different levels. To have the *suspicion* of betrayal is one level. It can drive you crazy, make you obsessive.

To have the *certain knowledge* of betrayal is like a blow to the chest, bruising your heart and making it seem impossible ever to get a clear breath again.

But the absolute worst is seeing or hearing or otherwise *witnessing* the betrayal.

With suspicion, you can hope you're wrong and your beloved has not in fact ever cheated on you—why did you ever doubt her or him, you fool. With certain knowledge, you can no longer hope it's not true, but you can at least imagine the best possible spin, that she went along with the betrayal reluctantly or that your husband was seduced by a shameless hussy; that through it all, your beloved was thinking of you and was crushed to be doing this awful thing to you, the one and only person he/she truly loved.

Ah. But when you see it or hear it for yourself, all the protective layers of self-delusion are stripped away and there it is, the ugly monkey-truth staring defiantly at you, as ugly as truth can be.

I don't think I took a breath during their entire long conversation. At one point she said she wished he would do something and he responded, "Your wish is my command." *And she laughed.* She was a literate person with a brilliant mind and he was a yokel with tiny little hands and a squeaky voice and he moved his lips when he tried to read, although in fact I have not confirmed that last assertion. One imagines.

The canoodling between them wasn't the worst part. If you know your soul mate is mating with another soul, you expect that there's going to be the requisite amount of tickle and giggle. What took my breath away was hearing them laugh at me. He said he was faking being my friend and coming into the house and letting me make coffee, hoping that this bogus friendship would put me off the trail of what was going on between the two of them. He thought it was funny, doing that. She said she was trying to talk me into going to New Orleans to do some more research on a book, hoping that with me out of town for a couple of weeks the two of them would have uninterrupted time together. But it's not working, he won't go, she said, *laughing*. He said he had a conference coming up and maybe she could get away and join him. She said that was a definite possibility. He asked if she still had the T-shirt he left for her. She said she wore it under her own shirt so she could smell and feel him next to her skin. My throat closed up so that, truly, I had to sit down and open my mouth and suck to get air. She asked if his wife had caught on that he came home without a T-shirt that day. They laughed about that, too—laughed at his wife. He told my wife that his wife had turned cold and they didn't have sex, didn't have satisfying sex. I wonder if any man in the history of cheating on a wife has ever *not* told the other woman that sex with his wife was absent or unsatisfying. And on and on went this conversation. It broke my heart.

A friend was visiting the day this happened, so I couldn't confront my wife until after our friend left. But I couldn't leave it alone, couldn't stop thinking about what I'd heard, playing the conversation over and over in my mind. One of my Guys in the Back Row was apparently Sicilian and he made explicit suggestions regarding what we should do about this breach of honor. Finally I told our friend he had to leave. He laughed. I said I was serious. He asked what was wrong. I said something's come up and you've got to leave. He did, pissed off.

I walked out to where she was cutting the grass on our riding mower. I smiled. She smiled back. I paused, appreciating the significance of this moment. We would never again have a normal conversation, just the two of us, without the beast present. I asked her who she loved. "Only you, baby," she said, smiling all the more.

I said I knew about her and the bastard she was cheating on me with. She denied it. Said I was being paranoid and foolishly suspicious. There was a certain thrill to this, I now admit. A thrill to knowing for a certainty that she was cheating but letting her believe I was only guessing—and to listen then to her earnest denials. I was torturing us both. I let her go on and on. The earnestness of her denials was so powerful that if I had not heard the telephone conversation with my own ear, I might have believed her denials. I knew about lies. I knew the role they played in making me crazy. Before I married my second wife I had become entangled with a beautiful woman who, I believe, was a pathological liar.

A pathological liar's need to lie goes beyond the usual reasons that motivate you and me to lie. If you're about to be caught doing something wrong, you might lie to protect yourself. Or if the truth will hurt someone, you might lie to protect that person. If a lie will make you seem more important (smarter, richer, a better lover), you might lie for aggrandizement. A pathological liar, however, apparently needs to lie for the experience of lying itself and, unlike the non-pathological liar, the pathological liar eventually needs for you to know—ideally, after the lie has been successful—that he or she has been lying.

When I lived with the beautiful pathological liar, the foot of our bed was against a wall, and one evening I came home to find that she had hung a picture on that wall. The photograph showed a close-up of her and a man. Both of them smiling. A lovely photograph. I asked why had she put it at the end of our bed. She said she found it while unpacking boxes and she thought it was a sweet picture, so she put it up in our bedroom to help personalize this apartment we had just rented. Did it bother me? she asked.

I should have tipped to her pathology at that moment. She was *acutely* interested in knowing if it bothered me. I said it was unsettling to see her smiling face next to some guy's smiling face . . . in our bedroom. She assured me that he was just a friend, that the two of them had never been intimate, had never even held hands or kissed. She assured me she would never have put up a picture in our bedroom of her with an ex-lover. She told me that she had many old friends, that she had loads of male friends, that in fact she liked male friends better than female friends, and that if I started getting suspicious and paranoid about every male friend she had, then we were going to have a rocky time together. This explanation was given with such force and sincerity and righteousness that I did not doubt her in the least.

Still, there was something unsettling about lying in bed at night and seeing the two of them smiling together at the foot of the bed before lights out. Or about making love to her with the lights on when she straddled me and I could glance at their smiling faces popping into view back there on the wall. When she threw her head back in ecstasy (faked or not—I can't even guess now) and collapsed on my chest, I got a good long look at the two of them smiling down upon me.

Although she *volunteered* the information that the two of them were only friends, never lovers, issues remained to nag at me. Why did she hang that picture and no others from her past? Why did she hang it at the foot of our bed instead of in the living room? I didn't press any of these matters. I thought I was being a sophisticated lover not to get hung up on her past.

Then something came up, another lie about this or that, an old friend who turned out to be an old lover, and in the middle of this new argument I said something elegant along the lines of . . . and the picture you hung over our bed, that was a guy you were fucking, too, wasn't it? It was. Someone she fucked within three hours of meeting him, she volunteered. I don't want to read too much into this, but she seemed sexually excited about being caught in this lie. I asked why would she put a picture of her and a lover over the bed she was occupying with me. She said she didn't know. Sometimes, she said, she just felt perverse.

I didn't ask her to take the photograph down, but the next day I saw it in the trash—photograph, frame, and broken glass. It seemed she had made her point, whatever that point was, and no longer needed the photograph to perform whatever little kink it was performing for her.

After I overheard my wife talking with her boyfriend, I asked questions and got caught in the tangled web that is spun to support an affair. I set traps, caught her fabricating. She kept to her story even if it defied logic.

Later I remembered all the times I lied to my first wife about where I had been and who I had been with—and the fear I had of being caught in a lie, but also the satisfaction that came from getting away with it. What goes around not only comes around, it comes around and jumps on your back and hurts you bad.

During the next several bad weeks, lies and detection of lies played out in the sleaziest possible ways. In all the years I had been with her, I had never checked on where she'd gone, never looked in her purse, never examined a phone bill. Not once. Now I was a pathetic Inspector Clouseau searching her dresser, going through her purse when she was outside, taking note of odometer readings, calculating how many miles she should have driven if in fact she had gone to where she said she'd gone.

"Where did you go while I was gone?"

"Nowhere."

"The odometer on the truck shows you went 6.7 miles."

"Oh, I went up to the store."

"For what?"

"A candy bar."

"Where's the wrapper?"

"The wrapper?"

"Yes, did you throw it away in the truck or here in the house or where?"

"I changed my mind."

"About what?"

"The candy bar. I picked it out and took it to the counter and then I decided I didn't need a candy bar, so I left it on the counter and drove home."

"You drove three miles to the store, picked out a candy bar, took it to the counter, left it on the counter, then drove three miles back home?"

"Yes."

"I don't believe you."

"Well, that's what I did."

It's hard to decide who was more pathetic in these exchanges. She had in fact gone to the store, I assume, to buy a phone card so she could call him without leaving evidence on our home phone, while I played Captain Queeg, obsessed not with missing strawberries but with a goddamn nonexistent candy bar.

She came home one afternoon after delivering a horse to a friend. As it happened, our friend called our house to talk to me and mentioned that my wife had just left for home. We had made that trip many times; it was forty minutes with a horse trailer. She didn't arrive home for another eighty minutes.

"What happened?" I asked when she got home.

"Nothing," she said. "Why?"

"You didn't stop to get something to eat? You didn't have truck trouble? A flat tire? You just drove right here?"

"Yes." Of course she didn't know I had been told the exact time when she left our friend's house. She asked why I wanted to know.

"Because Karl called and told me you were just then leaving their house and that was eighty minutes ago and the trip takes forty minutes. What happened to the missing forty minutes?" *Aha!*

She said she didn't know what I was getting at. She left our friend's house, drove straight here, and it took whatever time it took. "I was hauling horses so I had to take it slowly."

"The trip takes forty minutes *with horses*. In a car, it's less than thirty minutes. So unless you actually stopped or had trouble, forty minutes are missing."

She said I was crazy. I know I was *acting* crazy. And those missing forty minutes? It later came out that she was with him. Of course.

From Easter through summer, through the lies and denials and suspicions, bent by the weight of my ruined life, I eventually went as crazy as my mother ever was. I carried a gun, convinced he was going to come over to get her and try to kill me and I would have to defend myself by killing him first. I told her she would probably be killed in the crossfire. I told her I was using hollow-point cartridges. They make a hole the size of a pencil going in but then they blow out the back of your head. I asked her if she thought any jury would convict me for killing my wife's lover when he came on my property to meet with her.

"He's not coming here, David," she said quietly.

"Oh I think he is. And, believe me, I am so ready for that mother-fucker."

She looked at me with the sadness you feel for a friend lost to Alzheimer's.

I seldom slept. I drank pots of strong coffee. I stopped drinking gin.

The gin stoppage is significant. For the previous twenty years I had concluded just about every day of my life with at least two strong gin and tonics that put to rest the Guys in the Back Row and allowed me to turn off the voices created for my fiction. The routine was well established: coffee, write, gin, dinner, bed, sleep. But not during the madness. During the madness, I feared the very condition that I drank gin to achieve, a drowsy, sloppy, easy restfulness. During the madness, I had to stay on alert. She would try to go see him. He would try to come over to my house and see her. Then it got worse. She would try to kill me so she could be with him. No more eating anything she prepared. From Easter to Christmas that year, I would lose more than forty pounds. I shaved my head to ready myself for the coming battles.

Between manic sessions of paranoia and fear, I sank into depressions so severe that I felt utterly without hope or reason to live.

In William Styron's account of his slide into clinical depression, he laments that the word itself, *depression*, is too slight and too corrupted by common usage to carry the full weight and power of the disease it names. *I was depressed after the local team lost the big game.* Yes, you were depressed, but you weren't suffering from depression.

I was diagnosed with clinical depression, but I think a better name for what I felt is *anguish*—which I would define as an acute, intense, crippling feeling of anger, depression, paranoia, hopelessness, and a loss of impulse control tied to an incident, a tragedy, a loss, a betrayal. I think it should be called *clinical anguish*, differing from depression and madness but containing elements of both.

At the time of my anguish, my wife and I lived in a small brick ranch house, and I put a variety of locks on the door of my tiny office room. I began to sleep there rather than in our bedroom. Three locks on the inside of the door. And three locks on the outside so she couldn't sneak in when I wasn't there and sabotage the room. Locks on the windows. Every few days I drove to a mall and haunted the hardware aisles for more locks. Once I was asked to leave, I was alarming other customers. Once I was escorted out.

Hardware section of Wal-Mart.

"Can I help you, sir?"

"Looking for locks."

"All right. What kind of locks?"

"Big, strong locks for doors."

"You're whispering, I can't hear you."

"BIG STRONG LOCKS!"

"Okay, okay . . . our locks are on this aisle and the next one over. Are you okay?"

"She's just waiting for me to go to sleep. Then she's going to do it."

"Do what?"

"Exactly."

"Would you like us to call someone?"

"Who?"

"I don't know, sir. Someone who could come get you, drive you home. The other customers—"

"Oh, I see . . . she called here, didn't she?"

"Who?"

"Never mind your fucking locks . . . you'd be selling her duplicate keys anyway, wouldn't you?"

Being followed by security out to the parking lot.

Wal-Mart doesn't like crazy people.

I kept threatening to kill myself in my wife's presence. I put a .38 revolver to my head and wanted her to see me blow my brains out, but she turned away and left the room. When I shot a hole in the wall, she rushed back in to see if I had done it. I've never struck a woman in my life, but I beat up on her psychologically.

Then came the second awful night of my life, remarkably similar to the first one when I was twelve. At the conclusion of that second night I finally decided to kill myself. No more theatrics, no more shooting holes in a wall. No more threats. I wanted relief from the madness and the lies, and I knew where that relief waited.

13

AWFUL NIGHT NUMBER TWO, WHEN I WAS FIFTY-SEVEN

ALTHOUGH THE two awful nights of my life are separated by forty-five years, the same two themes were present at both—madness and a rage to kill. During the first awful night, my mother was crazy and my father wanted to kill her. During the second awful night, I went crazy and wanted to kill myself.

It started out as another night of anguish in our bitter end house in Tennessee. I was babbling some nonsense. The week before, I had shaved my head. I was carrying a gun, prepared for the assault. Sitting at our dining room table, I looked over at the front door. Quietly, terrified, my wife was trying to leave. She had our two dogs with her.

"Where are you going?" I demanded.

She shook her head. "You're scaring me too much, David . . . I have to leave."

"You're leaving me?"

"I have to. Before . . . something happens."

"I hid the car keys."

"I found the spares."

"You're not leaving me."

"David . . ."

"You did this to me . . . cheated on me . . . betrayed me at the low-est point of my life . . . and *you're* leaving *me*?"

"I have to."

I took the gun from the holster. A genuinely evil Guy in the Back Row, the one who usually sat hooded and grimly silent, stood and said, *Do it.* I felt a chill in my soul that came from the certain knowl-edge, I could do it. *Do it,* he said, you fucking coward, *do it.* I hated my father for bullying my mother and telling her he was going to kill her and now I became both of my parents, the murderously enraged one *and* the clearly insane one. Before the evil Guy in the Back Row could take control of my pointing arm, I quickly shot into the door frame . . . then collapsed on the dining room floor.

This wasn't theatrics to prevent her from leaving. I fainted or fell or could otherwise not keep myself upright. And as I hit the floor, I began wailing. My wife thought I had shot myself. I hadn't. I had gone mad. I remember the sensation of some rational part of me observing the proceedings with alarm.

The crazy Guys in the Back Row had mounted a successful mu-tiny, rushing to the controls and forcing the External Reality Team to step aside. It was that team, somber and appalled, who watched this scene unfold and waited to be called back in to take control again.

For now, though, the crazy Guys in the Back Row were in control, making me screech and crawl on all fours, my eyes rolling back in my head.

To her credit, my wife didn't leave as she probably should have. She stayed to deal with the mess her husband had become. But she didn't know what to do. She called friends of mine, trying to get me to talk to them. I refused the phone, wailing and crawling and put-ting my forehead on the floor. The dogs were appalled. They came to sniff me and then left. My wife wondered who to call. An ambu-lance? A cop?

She called both of my sons and was able to get through to the younger, Josh. She tried to give me the phone, but I still wouldn't or couldn't take it. When she forced it into my hand, I hung up. Josh called back. I don't know what he thought of his father in such anguish but he said the one thing with enough power and sense to stop me from killing myself later on that evening. Had he said, "I love you, Dad," I wouldn't have cared because it was love, an excess of love, that had put me on the floor that night. If he had said, "Things will get better," I wouldn't have believed him because I was convinced things were as bad as they had ever been in the history of the world.

Instead, he said the one thing that meant everything to me. He said, "I need you, Dad." Over and over. With my wife holding the phone to my ear as I crawled and babbled and screeched. I was every bit as crazy as my mother. "I need you. Dad, do you hear me—I need you." I was sobbing, screaming crazy talk about my wife trying to kill me, and Josh never tried to talk me out of anything I was saying, never said calm down, he just kept saying, "I need you." He must've said it a hundred times. "Dad, I need you." His statement played the one sane chord still intact in my mind, being run now by all the crazies from the Back Row. Even in this anguish, I still felt an obligation to my sons.

"I need you, Dad."

I told him I was a terrible person, she's going to kill me and I deserve to die.

"I need you."

I told him I was an awful father to him and his brother, that I was never there when they needed me, that I'm a failure.

"I need you."

I'm a failure at everything I've ever done, and now she's going to poison me, and then the man she's screwing around with is going to come over and live here because she hates me for being a failure, and she's going to kill me!

"Dad, I need you."

———

"I need you."

———

"Dad, I need you."

CONSIDERING SUICIDE

SHE LEFT after I hung up with Josh. I don't know where she went. Neither of us had any confidence about how the night would play out in the end. She was convinced one of us would die before it was over, maybe both of us. So she left and I went to my writing room and locked the three locks on the door and the two locks on the window and then I shut off the light so he couldn't get a shot at me through the window if she had gone to get him and bring him back here to finish the job I had failed to complete.

So here I sit on the edge of a single bed in a tiny room. I haven't slept in two days. Haven't eaten. Just coffee so I'm alert for when they come for me. I put a .38 revolver to my forehead. This is the single most exciting thing I've ever done in my life. Thrilling. If my heart was pounding and my hand shaking, it wasn't from fear of doing it. I was serene with the decision I'd made. The pounding-shaking came from the pure adrenaline rush.

I only wish she was here to see it, what she has wrought.

The revolver's muzzle to my forehead, I am careful to angle the barrel so the bullet will be sent deep into my brain and not just shoot off the top of my skull. For some reason, I felt compelled to shoot right between my eyes rather than into my mouth or to my temple. The summer before, I had shot a fawn between its eyes and it died instantly. A woman crying next to her car by the side of the road had flagged us down, explaining that she had hit the fawn and broken its back. It struggled in a ditch, squealing in pain, unable to stand. The fawn had to be put out of its suffering.

I wondered how much more madness I would suffer before being put out of it.

I began pulling the trigger. To understand what was happening, you need to know the difference between a single-action and a double-action revolver. With a single action, you have to cock the hammer first and then you can pull the trigger, releasing the hammer to fall on the cartridge. The trigger pull on a single-action revolver is fairly short and light because all you're doing is releasing the already cocked hammer. With a double-action revolver, the trigger pulls the hammer back and then, after reaching full extension, the hammer automatically falls on the cartridge. The trigger pull on a double-action revolver is consequently longer and heavier, because you are pulling the hammer all the way back before it automatically releases and the gun fires. With a double-action revolver, you can watch the hammer extend back as you pull on the trigger.

Sitting on a single bed in my writing room, behind multiple locks, with the double-action .38 revolver properly positioned against my forehead, I am *squeezing* steadily on the trigger, and with crossed eyes I can see the hammer slowly pulling back. People are in that room with me. People I know who have died. They are somber, waiting for my decision.

Trigger pull is measured in pounds. If six pounds of pull on that .38's trigger was sufficient to drive the hammer all the way back to the firing position, I had placed perhaps three pounds of pressure on the trigger, enough to take it halfway back. I was three pounds of trigger pressure away from blowing my brains out.

The first time I ever talked with Jon Carlock was at the doorway of a small Presbyterian church in Tennessee, just a couple miles from the farm where I lived with my wife. Jon had just preached the Sunday services. As my wife and I were leaving, Jon said he'd heard I was a writer and had sent away for my novel, *Pelikan,* which he had finished just the night before. I braced myself for what might come next— maybe this country preacher would ask me not to attend any future services. *Pelikan* is set in New Orleans and includes loving but profane descriptions of bars, prostitutes, would-be vampires, a trade in merkins, sexual perversions, and other enthusiasms that I thought would not sit well with a young preacher. But Jon leaned closer and whispered, "You and I share a worldview."

Turns out Jon is a professor at a small religious college and has one of the most eclectic points of view I've ever encountered. He's a gun and Corvette enthusiast, passes as a good ol' boy, and is intellectually curious about everything from hauntings to the formal study of philosophy. For some years now Jon has battled a central nervous system condition that can be devastating at times—but which he handles with uncommon grace. His wife, Myra, is as intellectually curious and funny as her husband but vastly more beautiful. She and I share our book addiction through e-mail, now that I've been gone from Tennessee for five years. If I had no one in my life except Jon and Myra, I'd have a rich life.

Jon is the one who finally disarmed me. The day after that awful night, my wife called him to come get my guns. And I agreed it was a good idea for all my firearms to be taken away from me. I gave Jon the rifle and shotgun and revolver, all of which he carried to his car. Then Jon and I sat awhile on a bench away from the house. Jon is passionate about his beliefs—and his friends—but ruthlessly unsentimental about life's realities. He didn't offer platitudes or prayers but said we had to get through this thing (the plural pronoun was not an affectation on his part) without anyone getting hurt, that was the main priority and that's why he was collecting my firearms. I said I understood. Jon said, "I won't let you kill yourself. And killing him won't end your problems either, will it?" I agreed that killing anyone would not solve any of my problems. Then he pulled out a little .25 semiautomatic of his own (I don't think Jon even goes to the shower unarmed) and offered it to me. "I don't like leaving a man *completely* unarmed," he said.

Which I thought was hilarious. "Jon, you come over here and take my rifle, you take my shotgun, you take my revolver—but you're giving me one of your own guns?"

"It's just a little .25 caliber," he said by way of explanation.

I told Jon that I thought being completely unarmed was a good condition for me at that particular time.

Jon then explained something that has stuck with me ever since. "Most people," he said, "would have to have devastatingly serious reasons to kill themselves. Others of us have to find good reasons each day *not* to kill ourselves."

I think people for whom suicide is not an option don't understand the distinction.

Franz Kafka said the meaning of life is that it ends. I remember the exact moment I understood that meaning. I was eight years old, sitting in the bathtub in the farmhouse where I grew up. A corner of my parents' bedroom had been partitioned off for an inside bathroom. (We wouldn't get phone service until I was sixteen years old but not having to use the outhouse, home to genetic mutant spiders, was joyous.) For some reason as I sat in the tub the idea abruptly occurred to me that one day I would be dead, would no longer exist, that the world would go on but I would be gone forever. I knew about death. I had helped kill a toad whose spirit even now awaits an explanation. But until that bath I apparently had never had the occasion to fast-forward and realize that, yes, someday I would die, too, and be erased from existence forever.

Even today I am surprised that we all go through life so docile in the face of this enormous reality. You'd think that mortality would make philosophers and poets of all of us.

I began to weep for the future loss of my life. No longer in existence for eternity! The old man either heard me crying or came in to find out what was taking me so long in the tub. "What's the matter?" he asked. I said, "Someday I'm going to die." He considered this a moment and then told me, "Someday we're all going to die . . . now get out of the tub."

Death loomed large in my consciousness three other times in my life. When I was a young man, I drank heavily, raced motorcycles, slept with married women whose husbands owned firearms, got into bar fights, and generally lived life like an asshole redneck whose last words are going to be "Hey, watch this!" I think I was confronting the fear of death I had as an eight-year-old by getting into death's face and saying, fuck you, take your best shot.

The next time death was on my mind was as I approached thirty and was afraid of dying without having published a book, becoming like the old man, an unpublished writer with a manuscript in the attic. So instead of daring death to take me, I began bargaining—just back off and let me finish this book, get it published, then I don't care if I die.

My third relationship with death, down in Tennessee, was completely different in that I no longer dared death or feared it, but desired its embrace. The eternal obliteration of my existence, which at one point terrified me, became a source of great comfort. With death, my depression or funk or hopelessness or anguish or whatever name it lurks by would be gone. Like the priest at the end of *The Exorcist*, I would embrace the evil and jump out the window to erase both of us.

And then what?

Heaven, of course.

Talk of heaven freaks out some people but it's been a comfort and a crutch to us poor people for thousands of years. Years ago, I spent an evening of drinking and dining and bar hopping with my friends Ambrose Clancy and Mary Lydon. We ended up at a bar called the Broken Down Valise.

Ambrose and Mary have accumulated a constellation of friends, and I count myself happy to be in that sky. We talk books and politics, but mainly we laugh. We once had a plan to start a vineyard on Long Island, and we realized that the most critical aspect for a successful vineyard was not financial backing or winemaking knowledge. No, it was coming up with a precious name. We spent one entire wine-fueled session considering and rejecting prospects—and then hit upon a beautiful and lyrical word that was perfect for our needs. We would call our vineyard: *Chlamydia Wines*. Motto: *Chlamydia—the wine that grows on you*. Our advertising campaign would encourage customers to request our wine by name: *Ask the nice people at your favorite restaurant or wine store*: *"Do you have Chlamydia?"* Alas, the dream of a vineyard collapsed when Ambrose ruthlessly grabbed the role of vintner for himself, leaving me to run the warehouse and take responsibility for the corks. Mary, of course, would have been president.

Our night together at the Broken Down Valise came after we had been out drinking for so long that I had drunk myself into and out of intoxication, achieving a level of mental clarity that was otherworldly. I spun for Ambrose and Mary my tale of heaven. No one is denied entry into this heaven because my God is a kind and generous and forgiving God. (If that doesn't match up to your avenging God who sends some of his beloved children to eternal damnation, then you should spin your own desperate tale of heaven and leave me to my comforts.)

In my heaven, I would have opportunities throughout eternity to speak with all the great writers. And they would have read my work. And some of them would have encouraging words for me. In my heaven I could go out drinking with Papa Hemingway. And I'd meet up with all the people I've known who've died and gone to heaven; some of them have been watching over me. I'd meet up with my old man who'd say something blustery and remind me of the old days: "You've heard of a soldier boy, haven't you, boy? And you've heard of a sailor boy, haven't you, boy? And you've heard of a flyboy, haven't you, boy? But you ain't never heard of a Marine boy—have you, boy?" And then he'd give me a thump to the chest and I'd say *oh Daddy I forgive you everything* and he'd call me his baby boy and ask me to recite it for him a few more billion times throughout eternity . . . *you'd scarcely expect a boy of my age . . .*

When the anguish hit me in Tennessee and I lost everything, I desperately and sincerely wanted to die. I didn't need the Broken Down Valise version of heaven to soften the blow or encourage the bullet. I just wanted out of life.

Some of the people I talked with who lost everything also felt that death—getting out of where they were—held a powerful appeal. These individuals were opposed to suicide on a variety of grounds but embraced *the possibility* of death. One woman had been physically abused by her husband for years, but he was a successful and respected member of their community and she thought no one would believe that this beloved figure was an abuser. And she feared that people would blame her for provoking him. He controlled all the family's finances. She couldn't get out of the marriage and she couldn't survive within it. She wouldn't even admit the truth to her own father. Driving along the highway one afternoon, she hit a patch of black ice and her car spun out of control. She told me she let go of the wheel and experienced a moment of profound serenity: I'm going to be killed and that, finally, will be the end of it. The car spun into a ditch but she wasn't injured. Realizing that she was actually desiring death gave her the courage to go to her father and tell him the truth and begin the process of getting away from her husband.

Another woman I know felt that she had lost everything when the man she loved died, and one morning on her way to work she accidentally stepped in front of a bus, jumping back on the curb at the last available moment. Instead of being rattled by this near-death experience, she thought it would have been okay if that bus had hit and killed her. Maybe she would be spiritually joined with the man who had died but, even if that was not the case, she would be free of the misery of this life.

I found this attitude again and again among people who had lost everything, who never attempted suicide, but who embraced the prospect of death.

The pertinent question is the one Jon Carlock posed—not why do people kill themselves but why do people who want to die *not* kill themselves.

Here are reasons I consider for not choosing suicide:

Suicide is a cruel legacy for someone else to deal with. And I'm not talking about the psychological aftermath exclusively but also the mess of finding the body and dealing with it. I suppose it wouldn't be so bad if you engineered a clean death brought on by pills, that occurred in your sleep, so that there's no blood or shit—but of course I was planning to blow my brains out, splatter them on the wall, collapse in a heap, and there I am, *you* deal with it, dearly beloved. For my sons to be called and told, your dad has blown his brains all over the bedroom wall—I would have to hate them to be so cruel to them.

Suicide can launch a family legacy that will take the lives of people not yet born. Research shows that once someone in a family commits suicide, the chances for others in that family to kill themselves—even many years later—increase. I think what happens is, when trouble comes and you lose everything, if another member of your family has killed himself or herself, even if you didn't know that person and just heard about it as family lore, the *option* of suicide has been put on the table. If no one in your family or no one close to you has ever committed suicide, then that possibility remains foreign. Maybe that's another reason I didn't pull another few pounds on that trigger that night—no one in my family that I know about has ever done it, so I had no precedent.

Life is over soon enough. In fact, life is so short that killing yourself is like falling out of an airplane without a parachute and then, on the way down, you blow your brains out. Just wait a little while and you'll be dead in any case.

But even with these arguments against suicide, even now that I've gained back much of what I lost, even now that I'm at peace with most of my life and can wish my ex-wife well with her new man— still, thoughts of killing myself are never far away. When something bad happens, a heavy disappointment with my books, for example, or when I get hit with a case of free-floating anxiety that frightens me and fills me with impending doom . . . I start to picture and plan and imagine how I could do it and how quickly all the bad shit would be over. But then I pull back and, as Jon says, I search for reasons to stay alive. I think I have a Guy in the Back Row who has become such a fatalistic son of a bitch that each time my life hits a bad spell, he jumps up and hollers, "That's it! Fuck it! Get the gun!" So far, in reaction to these outbursts, the External Reality Team has managed to quiet him, make him sit down, assured him that things will be fine. He shuts up for now, but I know that bastard is waiting there at the edge of his seat, ready to jump up and shriek his mortal advice the next time life seems unbearable.

I used to consider suicide cowardly. You should stay in the game and tough it out, was what I thought. But as with so many other insights I've gained through the experience of losing everything, I now understand that sometimes the load we carry makes it impossible for us to continue. I don't blame anyone who feels so trapped, hopeless, and crushed that suicide becomes a compelling option.

I know you have a thousand good reasons for killing yourself—and I would not argue with a single one of them. But maybe you'll find one good reason for staying alive today. If not, I hope for your sake that I'm right about a generous and forgiving God so you can end up in a heaven as appealing to you as the one imagined in the Broken Down Valise is to me.

None of these considerations of suicide saved me at the end of Awful Night Number Two, when I was fifty-seven, however. What saved me were those three words my son had said: "I need you." I sat there on the bed with the gun to my head. Josh needs me and Matt needs me, too.

I eased off the pressure and let the trigger gently reseat.

I wasn't going to kill myself, not that night . . . and not tonight.

On October 1, the same day I received these pages to proof, a sheriff's deputy in Pinellas County, Florida, found my sister's phone number in our brother's room and called. Eric had killed himself. Eric's demons, in pursuit for most of his adult life, had finally got him down and wouldn't relent, wouldn't let him get up ever again.

Eric was sixteen years younger than I am and ten years younger than Nancy. He was artistic, given to drama, and one of those men no one suspects is gay. He had been in a stable relationship for some years in New Orleans before Katrina hit. The house owned by Eric and his

partner had flooded but was not destroyed. After the hurricane, during a sustained upside of his manic-depressive cycle, Eric threw himself into restoring the house, having it raised on pilings, organizing the
neighborhood's homeowners, getting coverage for his actions in local
media and *The National Geographic.*

But Eric was a schemer. He associated himself with contractors of
dubious reputation, deals fell apart, insurance money was lost, and
Eric's general instability became less flamboyant and more tragic. He
started taking drugs. Meth, we think. One by one, he went through
his many friends, imposing on their hospitality, borrowing money,
and eventually having a falling out with each of them as he criticized
them, complained of their treatment of him, and sometimes said
things so hurtful that his friends refused all future contact.

This was an unfortunate pattern in Eric's life. Early on in a friendship, he would do anything for you—was funny and generous and
kind and supportive. You would think, I'll have no better friend in life
than Eric. And then something would change and you would want
him out of your life.

During one of his bumpy periods, he came to live with my wife
and me on our Blue Goose Farm in West Virginia. The early months
were glorious. He worked hard, kept track of his hours, we paid him
an agreed-upon wage, and he was able to regain his financial footing.
Eric was brilliant at just about everything he undertook—including
cooking. We had brilliant dinner parties with food prepared by Eric
and my wife, both of them drinking wine while opera blared so loudly
in the kitchen that they must have communicated using hand signals.
For one over-the-top dinner party, they slaughtered four ducks in the
morning, cooked all day, gathered wildflowers for the table, and eventually produced what we all thought was the finest experience, the
best food, the most laughing, we'd ever had in one evening.

But by the end of his stay with us, Eric had changed dramatically.
He kept to his room instead of working, although he still submitted
his hours to be paid. He told people we treated him like a slave. He
said we would call him while we were on the way home from a trip
and demand that he have dinner on the table by the time we arrived.
None of this was true, of course. Eventually my wife asked him to

leave—he had become such a depressive and negative influence in our lives.

Eric had a dear friend in New Orleans who put him up in her house for a year—but eventually she asked him to leave and then had all the locks in her house changed. With no place to stay, all his bridges burned, he broke into another friend's house in New Orleans while that friend was away on a trip. Alarms went off. Eric was arrested and went to jail.

During the past year, this last year of his life, he also stayed with a friend in West Virginia who loved him dearly until they had a falling out and she would have nothing more to do with him.

As his demons continued chasing him, Eric continued bouncing from optimism to depression. In his deepest troughs, he told people he was going to kill himself, and he sent streams of bizarre e-mails about being a savior, temples being built in his name, and a reckoning coming. Those of us who knew Eric had been hearing from him in these strange veins for so many years that we had become inured rather than alarmed.

Earlier in the summer, my sister Nancy was visiting a friend in Florida and had rented a place near the ocean when she received yet another call from yet another friend of Eric's, saying that our brother was in trouble again. Eric eventually called Nancy and said he was at the end of his rope, and she told him he could join her in Florida. She rented an apartment for him, helped him buy things he needed, paid for three months' rent, and told him he could get a job, take over the rent, and start rebuilding his life. Following his usual pattern, he began by expressing his devotion and love and gratitude to his sister and ended up by saying vicious things to her.

She returned to the house that she and I share in Virginia, leaving Eric in Florida to pull himself together now that he'd been given another chance for a fresh start. He befriended the landlord and his wife, becoming their instant best friend in the usual Eric fashion. But he never got a job—and never found a way to escape the demons.

A couple of weeks before he killed himself, he called me and asked if he could come to Virginia and stay with Nancy and me. I said no. I said there was no work here, that he had a better chance of finding a job where he was. Nancy had told me there were restaurants near the apartment in Florida, plenty of places to find a job. Eric had once upon a time been a successful waiter, had even co-owned a restaurant with Nancy for a while. During our last phone conversation, he told me he couldn't pay the rent. He said that after he was evicted he would become homeless. I said I was sorry. We had all received these pleas from Eric over the years. Friends who took him in eventually had to ask him to leave. I wasn't going to participate in the pattern again. I was a hard-ass. He was forty-six years old. Nancy and I both believed that people taking him in and supporting him had contributed to his dependency, his inability or unwillingness to get a job and live independently.

He showed us. He had bought a gun the month before. He covered all the mirrors in his apartment. He put a note on the door, telling the landlord, his new friend, not to come in but to call the police instead. Eric went into the bathroom, into the shower, and put towels down to contain the mess. He shot himself under the chin. Apparently no one heard the gun.

The situation became just about as ugly as it could become. A terrible stench was coming from Eric's apartment. Flies covered the windows. A neighbor eventually called 911. My brother had been dead several days in the Florida heat before the detective discovered his decomposing body.

In this final, passive-aggressive act, our brother bequeathed us guilt and a mess that we had to deal with long-distance while the landlord and police and medical examiner and biohazard cleaning service had to handle it in person. And our brother left us with questions and doubts. Could we have done something to change the course of his life and death? Were we wrong to tell him to get a job and start taking care of himself and stop expecting others to come to his rescue? Should Nancy have sent him even more money? Should I have said, yes, brother, come stay with us?

During my bad night, five years before Eric killed himself, I came *that* close to doing what Eric did, but I was lucky because I knew my sons needed me, and maybe Eric thought no one needed him.

Let me end with the belief that Eric did not in fact kill himself thinking, *that will show them . . . how I was hurting . . . how much I needed their help.* Let me, instead, believe that his death was caused by those internal demons that got him on the ground and tore into him—and death was the only peace he could achieve, the only relief he could find from pushing and pulling all that *stuff* we accumulate through life. Eric, you poor, troubled soul—rest in peace.

PART III

*Losing Everything Is Not What Breaks
Your Heart; What Breaks Your Heart Is
Trying to Hold On to What Is
Already Irretrievably Lost*

In each disastrous instance—from financial to marital—the damage caused by the actual loss was secondary compared to the damage and heartbreak and frustration caused by trying to save what was already lost.

If I had admitted early on that my career as a full-time, well-paid novelist was over, I could have recovered. I could have had a regular job and then worked on my books in the evenings, on weekends, as I do now. It was trying to hold on to a career, *already* lost, that led me into debt and allowed me to drift in stupid hope of being rescued.

If I had let go of our status as middle class or well off, a status that was already decidedly lost, then I wouldn't have bought a mansion in Saratoga Springs that we were forced to sell after it had vacuumed the remains of our savings.

If I had given up on my marriage when I knew it was lost, I would have been hurt, desolate even, but I would not have driven myself crazy, would not have tortured my wife with accusations and surveillance, would not have lost *all* my dignity.

By not accepting the reality that the marriage was over, I became like a mad doctor who keeps trying to revive a corpse, who keeps resuscitating and pumping and shocking, and nothing works because *the person is already dead* and it is clear to everyone that the efforts to revive are pathetic, insane.

I knew everything was dead. The writing career. The money. The marriage. But I kept desperately trying to make those corpses live again.

People have said this is a defeatist attitude, that I'm basically saying, Give up. But that's not what I'm saying at all. Trying to hold on to what is already lost is what defeats you. In my extended family is a smart, attractive, vivacious woman whose husband regularly and publicly humiliates her, but she holds onto that marriage out of some sense that it gives her status and financial comfort and social standing. But that marriage is already over, her social standing is already lost—and regular humiliation is the price she pays for continuing to hold to what is already lost.

Someone asked me how you know if something is already irretrievably lost as opposed to something that is in jeopardy but can still be saved.

You know. You can skew the evidence. You can pretend. But you know. Think back on a time in your life when something fell apart and eventually you lost it—don't you remember when you knew it was lost, when you knew it couldn't be saved? You knew it was gone, but you kept trying to hold on to it and that was the part that broke your heart.

I knew she wore his T-shirt next to her skin so she could feel and smell him, I heard her say that to him, and yet I still tried to hold on to that marriage and make it live again.

| 5

HITTING BOTTOM

AFTER THAT night I went crazy but did not kill myself, I left Tennessee and drove to Washington, D.C., to stay with one of my sons. My older son, Matt, said he would rent a larger apartment so the two of us could live together, and my younger son, Josh, said I could stay up in the attic room of the house that he and his wife, Kathy, owned. I can't remember how we reached that decision for me to leave Tennessee. I think my wife talked with my sons, who talked with me. I didn't want to go. I was convinced that as soon as I was out of state, she would resume her affair with *him*. When I told her this, my wife said, "Don't be ridiculous. You've so terrified him he wouldn't come within a mile of me."

I had, in fact, put the fear of God into the small-handed little bastard with the squeaky woman's voice. I had written him letters warning him to stay away and I made phone calls and I went over to his house to talk to him. I never caught him at home; I think that was because his girlfriend called to warn him I was on my way over. He eventually went to the county attorney, who wrote me a letter, saying that the man had promised he would stay away from my wife and I should just back off and leave this matter alone. I wrote the county attorney and said okay, I wouldn't contact the man again if everyone was telling me the truth about no future involvement with my wife. And that's what everyone promised me—my wife, the man, the county attorney. That there would be no more contact. Nothing the man or the county attorney or my wife told me turned out to be true, however. The man resumed his affair with my wife after I'd been out of state for a couple of months.

I arrived at Josh's and Kathy's house near Old Town Alexandria in the summer of 2003 with the possessions that could fit in my car and a small rental trailer. After a lifetime of work, I was in my mid-fifties traveling with everything I owned. The car was worth less than I owed on it, and I couldn't come up with the difference, so I had to keep it and continue making payments on it. I've never defaulted on an obligation in my life, but at that point I was $60,000 in debt with no prospects.

My two sons and daughter-in-law greeted me and each of them said they would have passed me on the street and not recognized me. I had lost forty pounds and shaved my head.

I had to get a job and go to a doctor to start treatment on the diabetes that was killing me.

Doctors first. I had several examinations, putting the cost on the last credit card I was able to use. I was diagnosed with diabetes and given prescriptions. I was also diagnosed as clinically depressed but refused that medication.

One of the side effects of the medicine I had started taking was constipation. My bowels were also affected by stress, the worries of being unable to find a job, doubts about my wife back in Tennessee. The upshot was, I became massively constipated. *But wasn't aware of it.* Wasn't paying attention. Too much else on my mind to realize that a week had gone by, and then two weeks, and then three without ever having an adequate bowel movement.

(Those of you who have problems with scatology should skip ahead to the next chapter as we turn now to some serious shit.)

What happened was, the fecal matter lower in my intestines became impacted and wouldn't move out and wouldn't let anything get by either. So the "good" feces, all soft and passable, was being dammed up behind the "bad" feces, all solid and paste-like. As the good feces kept building up, it finally decided something had to give—and called forth contractions. I began suffering from abdominal pain worse than any physical pain I'd ever had, a series of contractions that weren't accomplishing anything because of the impacted blockage. Aware finally that something was desperately wrong, I decided to resolve matters by taking a powerful laxative. This made everything terribly worse. The laxative put massive pressure on the feces that was trying to get by, through, around the impacted blockage. A bowel obstruction like I had can put enough stress on the body to cause death—a heart attack or bowel perforation.

After taking the laxative, I went to see a cowboy movie with my son, Matt. In the middle of it, the pain became so severe that I had to leave the theater. Back at Josh's and Kathy's house, I thought I could tough it out. I thought eventually I would go to the bathroom and get relief. But the pain became progressively worse and there was no relief to be had on the commode so, mortified, I had to knock on their bedroom door and ask them to take me to the emergency room. I don't go to doctors. Seeing an endocrinologist about the diabetes was the first time I'd been in a doctor's care (other than for insurance examinations and during my time in the Air Force) since I had had my tonsils out at eight. But this was serious. Josh and Kathy knew it was serious because I would not volunteer to go see a doctor unless I thought I was dying.

The emergency room was jammed. The pain came in waves, like what I imagine birth contractions are like. But even between the waves I was in constant pain as the laxative-empowered feces tried to bully its way past the three weeks of impacted feces blocking escape.

Nurses at the emergency room triage everyone who comes in to identify who has to be treated right away and who can wait. I don't know what my blood pressure and pulse rate were, but the numbers were sufficiently high to alarm the admitting staff into thinking I was about to have a heart attack. I was immediately put on a gurney and rushed past a dozen or more waiting patients to my own examining room.

I was told to take off my clothes and put on a paper hospital gown that closes, though not completely, in the back. The pain was horrible. It crumpled me into a fetal curl. It made me cry out involuntarily. And unlike an expectant mother, no one crowded around me, patting my shoulder and telling me when to breathe and when to pant and when to push. No one wanted to see this baby I was trying to have.

In fact, once the source of my discomfort was known, no one on the emergency staff wanted much to do with me. I don't blame them, especially not after something happened, so alarming and embarrassing that I hesitate to describe it. The pressure behind the blockage became powerful enough that rivulets of liquefied feces made their way through the blockage and squirted out of me, beyond my control.

The bathroom for the emergency room was down a corridor flanked by curtained-off examining stations. At some stations, the curtains were open and whoever was in there on a gurney could see me. Also, the corridor was crowded with doctors and nurses and aides and police officers and patients going in and out of the examining stations. I had to make my way through this Grand Central Station of activity holding the paper gown together in the back, and what's worse—terribly, terribly worse—I'm shitting myself along the way. Once in the bathroom, I tried to evacuate my bowels but the blockage would not be moved despite having been breached by pencil-thick streams of liquid shit. I made a mess. I was mortified. I stuffed paper towels between the cheeks of my ass to plug the leakage as best I could. The only benefit of the excruciating pain was that it blocked normal embarrassments about private body issues. In other words, it hurt so bad that while I kept apologizing to people for shitting everywhere, I was more obsessed with the pain than I was with my ongoing mortification.

I imagined that the External Reality Team was in an embarrassed tizzy, ordering apologies, offering pained expressions to the hospital staff around me—while the Guys in the Back Row kept shouting, *Fuck the apologies, we are fucking dying here!*

I was taken to be X-rayed. Pushed on a gurney, down the busy corridor, into an elevator, down to radiology, shitting as I went. When I was helped off the gurney, I had left my signature brown stain. "I'm so sorry." The pleasant ladies in radiology were sympathetic, helping me stand where I had to stand, helping me back on a fresh gurney, and cleaning up after me wherever I went. I tried to explain that I had no control over it, it just came out.

One of the attendants, a nice middle-aged lady, said I should eat prunes and psyllium husks. I asked her, "If I did that right now, would this clear up?"

She seemed alarmed. "No," she said, "I was talking about a diet you can follow to prevent this from happening again. Nothing in your diet is going to help you *now*. The X-ray shows you're completely blocked. They might have to operate."

Operate? No! I want to have this child naturally! No caesarean to remove this difficult baby, please, no.

I was wheeled back to my examining cubicle. A nurse's aide, a lovely young black woman, came in with a plastic tube and bag of saline, explaining that she was going to insert the tube into my rectum and then introduce the saline into my bowels under the theory that this would liquefy the blockage and allow it to pass. We looked at each other. She was clearly more reluctant about this procedure than I was. At least I could look forward to the hope of relief, while all she could look forward to was inching a tube up a crazy old white man's ass. I said, "I'll tell you what. I'll take the tube and the bag down to the bathroom and I'll do it to myself."

Her face brightened . . . then she wasn't so sure. Could I really do it by myself? I assured her I could. I told her I had been a corpsman in the Air Force. Convincing her to let me do it wasn't that difficult.

Off I go down the still-busy corridor, one hand holding the paper gown closed behind me, the other hand carrying the tube and bag. In the bathroom, I managed to do what I was supposed to do, but the procedure brought no relief. The water wouldn't go in because the blockage blocked the tube's opening until I pushed the tube farther inside of me, until it passed the blockage, and the saline solution could flow in *above* the blockage, adding its weight and pressure to all the weight and pressure already there. In other words, it made things worse. When I explained this failure to the nurse's aide, she said I should try again because liquefying the blockage is the only remedy available short of an operation. I said I'd give it another shot; the tube was still in the bathroom, all I needed was another bag of saline solution. She said I could fill the bag with tap water because, all things considered, we weren't really worried about keeping things sterile down there, were we?

I tried again, putting in more water above the blockage, creating an even greater pressure, the cramps more severe—I wanted to die. I wasn't able to urinate, either, and the pressure increased until at one point I was convinced that my bladder was going to burst. The nurse's aide brought in a catheter. I had catheterized patients when I was in the Air Force, but I didn't remember the catheter being the size of a freaking garden hose. This was one procedure I would not, could not, do to myself, so for the first time in my life I was catheterized. It took my breath away. And the amount of urine the procedure produced was modest, not a bladder-busting quantity. Turns out that the blockage in my bowels and the buildup of material had put so much pressure on my bladder that it felt like it was overly full when in fact it was simply being crushed and squeezed like a plastic bag.

Three agonizing hours. The nursing shift changed. New people came in, checked the chart, looked at me, smiled thinly, then left. I decided I would go home to my son's house and die in privacy. I looked around and found my clothes and started to get dressed but was interrupted by an angel.

She was beautiful and exotic, perhaps from Indonesia. Thin with large bright dark eyes and long black hair. "Where are you going, Mr. Martin?" she asked, having checked the chart for my name.

"Home. Nothing's working. I might as well be home. I'll take the tube and bag and keep trying that."

"Please sit down and remove your clothes." She told me she'd seen the X-rays. "Your blood pressure and heart rate are still dangerously high, you can't leave until we take care of this."

"How are we going to take care of it?"

"First, you're going to drink this . . . the whole bottle."

"What is it?"

"A strong laxative."

I shook my head. "Taking a laxative is what set all this mess in motion. I'm blocked up. Nothing can get past it. Putting more stuff in, adding more pressure, all that just makes the cramps worse."

"We're going to take care of that."

Why did she keep saying *we* were going to *take care* of it?

I drank the laxative, the whole bottle. It tasted like salty 7-Up.

The doctor said the laxative would take its full effect in about an hour.

Great. In an hour I'm going to have cramps that will cause my toenails to drop off. Jokes occurred to me—Doc, do you think we can save this child?—but I was too wracked by pain to find anything remotely funny.

"Turn over on your side," the beautiful doctor said softly, pulling on latex gloves.

"What're you going to do?" In my heart of hearts I already knew, had already suspected the moment she promised we would take care of this problem.

"I'm going to go in and remove the blockage. Most of it is right there where I can reach it."

"Oh, Doctor," I said. I remember exactly what I told her. "You didn't go into medicine for this."

She said something about taking the good with the bad. I was the bad, of course, we both understood that.

I still hadn't lain down or turned to my side. She said, "If we don't take care of this, it could kill you. The bowel obstruction could cut off blood supply to the bowel, lead to bowel strangulation. It won't be pretty and it could be deadly."

I imagined my funeral. Sad-eyed friends speaking softly, one asking the other, "I heard he died in the emergency room but what exactly was wrong with him?" And the other friend replying, "He was full of shit." And both of them laughing their fool heads off. Come on, Clancy, you profane bastard, you know you'd be making "Martin was always full of shit" comments. I decided I should die of something else. As Scarlett pledged not to be hungry again, I pledged not to die full of shit.

I lay on the gurney and turned to my side. My beautiful angel squirted KY Jelly all over her gloved hand.

When my wife and I owned a working farm, the vet would check a cow's pregnancy by pulling on a plastic sleeve that went all the way to his shoulder, liberally covering that sleeve with a lubricant, and then putting his hand and arm up the cow's rectum. Once inside, he could palpate the cow's uterus from her bowel.

And now *my* doctor was going to check on *my* baby in a similar fashion. But her intrusion would be much more modest than a vet's, I was sure. Just a finger. Maybe two. And while inserting her slender digits up my bum, she'd undoubtedly lay her other hand softly on my shoulder and purr encouragement, *that's it, yes, we're taking care of this, aren't we, yes we are . . .*

Yet, if this was going to be a modest intrusion . . . then why was she lubricating her whole entire gloved hand like a vet preparing to go up a cow? Surely she wasn't planning to put her entire . . .

Gathering several surgical pads to collect the newborn, she walked behind me and proceeded to put her entire hand up my ass. No, seriously. Her entire hand went up my ass.

It hurt. I was violated. She didn't bother telling me to relax because this was beyond relaxing. She just did her job. In spite of me. She went in after shit regardless of what any of my sphincters did to stop her.

It was so bad that my hand instinctively reached around behind me and tried to grab her arm. I didn't do this consciously, but one of the Guys in the Back Row was screaming, "She's putting her fucking hand up our ass!"

My beautiful invading MD didn't order me to cease, she simply used her free hand to grab my wrist and prevent me from stopping her. We struggled like that for several long moments, my hand reaching around to fight her as she fended me off with one hand and continued digging for shit with the other.

When it was over—I was breathing heavily, sweating, exhausted—she wrapped the bundle in the surgical pads, unpeeled her gloves and added them to the bundle, which she then carried to the hazardous waste container. I was tempted, and I'm not saying this to be funny but was really tempted, to ask if I could see the poor thing I had just birthed with the doc's help.

"It's over, then?" I asked as I gingerly sat up, wincing.

"No," she said.

No?

"There's a lot more up there."

Twins!

She continued, "But I think I've cleared the blockage so that the rest of it can pass when that laxative takes effect within the hour. I'll give you an enema kit that you can take with you and give to yourself when you get home. It should help."

"How can I ever thank you."

She smiled but we didn't shake hands.

I knew I'd never see this beautiful angel again, but I felt a certain poignant connection with her.

I dressed and came limping out of the emergency room to the waiting area where my son, Josh, and daughter-in-law, Kathy, were still waiting, even though the hour was toward midnight by then and both of them had work the next day. On the way home (I had them spread towels on the seat so I wouldn't foul their car), I gave a general outline of what had happened but I left out the part about a twin that hadn't been born yet, that I still carried within me.

After Josh and Kathy went to bed, I entered the bathroom, lay in the tub, and administered the enema. But I didn't mount the throne. Not yet. There had been too many disappointments that night. Too many failed attempts. I wasn't going to try again until I was sure of success.

Within the hour, just as my angel had promised, the rumblings began in earnest and after a short but vicious struggle I passed the other twin. No doubt about the paternity of that little bastard. And then soon enough, everything behind it came out in torrents of shitty afterbirth. I figured that the total, including the twin who never came home from the hospital, was close to ten pounds. The next morning I felt like a fashion model, hollowed out.

LOOKING FOR WORK
WITH A SHAVED HEAD AND A
TWENTY-YEAR GAP IN THE RÉSUMÉ

THE DAY after my bowel obstruction, one of my molars broke off at the jaw and I had to rush to a dentist for an emergency repair job. I cracked that tooth biting down too hard during the birthing process.

I had hit bottom. My writing career dead. My wife cuckolding me. My health shot to shit. Living in my son's attic room. $60,000 in debt. No job. No prospects.

I think the reason I've included so much nasty detail here about the bowel obstruction—other than the fact that I am a nasty man—is that the condition I suffered symbolizes perfectly the bottom, so to speak, that I had hit. I had come close to dying not by my own hand, not tragically, not young, not famously—but had almost died an embarrassment, full of shit. Of course. My death a joke to cap a life that had wasted so many opportunities.

Recovery would have to be through a job, through the dignity of work. This is what the old man had always drilled into me: you can outwork the bastards. I didn't care what the job was, changing tires or writing speeches. I was one skinny, shaved-head, bowel-unobstructed, old fart who was ready to work.

I had an old suit cleaned and started going on job interviews. People who glanced at my e-mailed résumé and didn't immediately discern the twenty-year gap in regular employment were eager to see me. I'd been a magazine editor with a staff of nearly twenty reporting to me, and I'd been a vice president for publications at a major foundation. But then they saw me in person and were appalled, some of them not even trying to hide their disappointment. They had assumed I was in my early forties with twenty years experience but I was approaching sixty with twenty years experience working in regular jobs and another twenty years working as a full-time novelist and farmer.

There were other issues that I became aware of only in retrospect. I had lost forty pounds, so my shirt and suit coat were too big for me; my hair was growing out from having shaved my head. Add all that to the twenty-year gap in my résumé, and I'm sure now that interviewers thought I was just getting out of prison.

I made them nervous. Seeing their anxiety, and being two decades out of practice often made me a basket case during the interviews. I interviewed at a small association representing rural interests, which I thought would be perfect for me considering my farm background. The woman who interviewed me was large. Not just overweight but massive. She asked me what I thought of working for an organization with just a few employees. I said I thought that would be a good thing. "Better to be small and nimble," I said blithely, "rather than having so many employees that your organization becomes a fat, bloated bureaucracy." She raised her eyebrows . . . oh my God, I just realized what I said but of course I couldn't then say that I didn't mean anything by what I had just said because commenting on it would make the situation worse. After that, everything that came out of my mouth seemed to carry a double meaning. How did I enjoy farming? "We had some lean years but we had some fat ones, too." What did I think of the role nonprofits play? "I have *enormous* respect for them." And each time I said something like this, I would get a stricken expression on my face as I realized what I was doing. At one point, she got up and opened the door to the interview room—I think so she could shout for assistance when I finally went bat-shit crazy as I was so clearly about to do.

I applied for dozens of jobs and went on a dozen interviews. When it became clear that I wasn't going to get an editorial position, I tried to get a job as a caretaker on an estate, but they didn't want a novelist, not even one with two decades of experience with farm equipment.

When I left the world of regular employment, computers were just becoming standard equipment and e-mail hadn't taken off as the method of business communications. If I last worked *before* computers and e-mail, who the hell was going to hire me?

I worked at a temp agency that took me on because of my blinding typing speed and the fact that I earned one of the highest scores the company had ever recorded on the editorial test for administrative assistants (a position that the world had stopped calling secretarial in my absence). But even the temp work was scarce.

I applied for beginning jobs paying less than half of what I had been making twenty years before. I aimed higher and applied for management jobs. University jobs, teaching creative writing—but without at least a master's of fine arts, I couldn't get colleges and universities to accept my applications; they didn't care how many books I'd written. I aimed lower, trying to get a retail job, a job at a bookstore, for chrissakes, the job posted in the window and paying minimum wage, but I didn't get that job either. Having written ten novels and loving books and knowing books wasn't sufficient to overcome my ex-con appearance and my lack of retail experience.

I would've been a great employee. I can write anything—speeches, annual reports, brochures. I'm a fast writer. Hard worker. And I would have been so thankful for the job that I wouldn't have talked back or ridiculed the company fight song or said no to anything I was asked to do. I had my mind right.

But what you discover in the business world is that employers are looking for workers who fit certain molds, and the employers would rather hire a candidate who fits that mold but isn't particularly skillful than to take a chance on an exquisitely skilled candidate who doesn't fit the mold, who might not be *like the rest of us*. It's also about covering your ass. They don't want some higher-up coming to them in six months and saying, "This Martin character you hired, the one who went crazy and created all the disruption in the workplace, I'm just curious . . . did you notice anything dicey about him during his interview . . . any gaps in his employment record, for example, or did he maybe look a little crazy in the eyes?"

As the months went by, I became increasingly alarmed by the thought of what would happen to me if I *never* got a job.

The friend I've known longest in my adult life is Barbara Parker, and when I returned to D.C. she took me under her protection and guidance. She paid for dinner when we went out because she had a job and I was broke. She told me about a friend of hers, Carl Luty, who was hiring an editor/writer at the Fannie Mae Foundation.

Carl is about my age, a year younger. He's worked on political campaigns, was a college professor, wrote speeches for top executives— but here's the key attribute that led to my eventual employment: Carl just didn't give a fuck about following the rules, fitting people into molds, and covering his ass. He told me later that he didn't want to interview me because if he didn't hire me, Barbara would be pissed at him. It would be easier to tell her the job search was closed. But for some reason he went through with the interview. And didn't care about the gaps in my résumé. And wasn't put off by my gaunt look and prison haircut. In fact, he thought it would be fun to have a novelist on the staff. He wasn't threatened by me. So he told me he was going to hire me; we just had to wait for the selection process to be completed officially.

This was life-changing. But as I was waiting to hear that I officially had the job, I found out that Carl had collapsed on the golf course. Great. Just at the moment of my salvation, the son of a bitch who is saving me has a heart attack. I speculated about rushing to the hospital and finding out if he said anything to anyone about hiring me before he kicked the bucket—something concrete I could take to HR, his last words on earth maybe . . . *hire Martin*. But happily for me (and Carl), he didn't die. His health problem turned out to be a minor issue with potassium levels that caused him to faint and he was soon back to work . . . and he recommended hiring me just as he said he would.

I still had to go through the interview process with the higher-ups, with Carl's boss and Carl's boss's boss. These were supposed to be routine, the job was mine to lose. To survive the formality of these final interviews, all I had to do was smile at the right parts, be serious at the right parts, and don't do anything stupid that the Guys in the Back Row might suggest. I had a talk with the External Reality Team. You're in charge. You should never have allowed the crazy Guys in the Back Row to take over in Tennessee. Don't let it happen again. No matter what they say, don't get distracted.

Carl's boss, Beverly Barnes, looked at my résumé and said, "I don't care why you are applying for a job that you're obviously over-qualified for, I just care that you do the job you're hired to do." I promised I would.

Beverly's boss was Stacey Stewart, at that time president and CEO of the Foundation, and I didn't say anything crazy in her office, either.

I was hired! Working there turned out to be a life-affirming three-year sanctuary. I took on a second job, freelancing editorial work. I was able to pay off my debts and start saving money. More important than the financial healing, however, was the kindness of the people I worked with.

Christina Tucker was writing her first novel and we talked about writing. Laurie Strongin was writing a book about the death of her son, Henry, and we talked about how difficult it is to write plainly on topics so complicated by emotion. Down in the technology cave, Lewis Christian and I listened to jazz during our lunch breaks and sometimes Brent Harshberger joined us. Donna Purchase and I worked together on Help the Homeless programs. People were lovely.

Some employees said the Foundation was a crazy place to work, and I suppose there was the usual amount of misunderstanding and power play and other crap that occurs in any work environment. But to me, it was close to heaven. A job! The boss-boss, Stacey Stewart, was beautiful and smart and had great instincts for what motivates people and for how the power structure works. Carl's boss, Beverly Barnes, was brilliant and beautiful and hilarious. I got to go to work in a clean, dry, well-heated place where I worked among beautiful women and stalwart men. What was not to love?

The two colleagues I remained closest to were Carl Luty and Kathy Litzenberg. Kathy once told me that success is a matter of luck, tenacity, attitude, and talent. The loss of any one of these can sink you. But if you have all four, success is assured. I keep trying to figure out which ones I'm missing.

The three of us went out to lunch together, had intense gossip sessions behind closed doors and used the hallways to see if we re-membered how to skip. We got along famously, worked together smoothly, produced good stuff for the Foundation, and had so many laughs together that even at the time we knew we'd look back with great fondness.

I left Tennessee in July 2003, searched for work for four months, started at the Foundation in November, but didn't stop being crazy until well into 2004. I kept calling my wife to see how she was doing, to check up on her. Why wasn't she home when I called her, where had she been? Ridiculous! I didn't know where she was or how she was meeting him when I lived there at the house with her; how in God's name did I expect to hold onto to her or do anything about whatever she was doing if I was a thousand miles away? But I kept desperately clinging to what was already irretrievably lost. I was still crazy about her and over her. The idea of her being with another man was a constant torture. Whatever Guy in the Back Row was in charge of bringing up those images was a perverse genius, painting pictures vivid enough to prevent me from sleeping, from thinking, from writing.

Eventually my wife told me everything. I supposed I had been tormenting her for the truth for so long that she finally decided I de-served exactly what I had been asking for. She told me that when I was living there with her in Tennessee, she and her boyfriend would arrange to meet at the side of a country road barely out of sight of our house. And he would come over to shoe her horses and they would go behind the barn and make out like teenagers. They met once with their respective trucks and horse trailers on the lot of a closed business outside Paris, Tennessee, and a police officer caught them. After I left that summer, she repeatedly called him and eventually convinced the pipsqueak to come over and resume and consummate their affair in spite of promises he had made to the county attorney. The man was unsettled by the possibility that I might find out about his return, and he was unable to perform.

Only one detail in her account did not break my heart.

In the middle of all this, my wife was diagnosed with breast cancer, and we decided to stay married until it was treated, which took a year. I asked if I could come see her while she was undergoing treatment, but she said it would be better if I didn't. She was sweet enough to say that seeing me and then watching me leave again would be too painful. But I suspect the truth was she had promised him I would not return to Tennessee.

It's strange to think that the woman I love so deeply went through a year-long bout with cancer and I never saw her, not even once. We talked regularly. She sent me pictures after she had shaved her head following hair loss from the chemotherapy and radiation. I wanted to go see her even though she had explicitly asked me not to come down there and more than once I planned a trip—but then never followed through. She had told me that one of the problems that developed toward the end of our marriage was the way I would take over and make all the decisions: move to Florida, move to Saratoga Springs, move to Tennessee. And if I made the decision to come visit her when she asked me not to, wasn't I still being overbearing? Or was I staying away to avoid dealing with her illness?

Some aspects of losing everything I've figured out, others I haven't.

In the end what finally made me stop being crazy about her was the simplest thing in the world: time. I read once that Romans arranged to have a slave whisper a sentence into the emperor's ear at times of great triumph *and* at times of massive defeat. And it was the same sentence in both triumph and defeat: *This too shall pass.*

When she completed her treatment and was given a clean bill of health, we agreed to divorce.

Elisabeth Kübler-Ross outlined five stages that people go through when faced with grief and catastrophic loss: denial, anger, bargaining, depression, acceptance. Kübler-Ross said that the steps don't always proceed in order but that a person losing everything always goes through at least two of the five. I didn't go through denial, got more than my share of anger, skipped bargaining, and made up for it with lots of depression. But acceptance?

I don't know. I've talked with people who've suffered devastating losses and I'm sorry to report that happy endings in the form of acceptance are hard to come by. Some of the people I've talked with aren't sure if they can ever be truly happy again for the rest of their lives. The most common and lasting feeling they have is *longing*. Missing the person. Missing the marriage. Missing the life they once had. And the best they ever hope for is that the longing eventually becomes bearable. Not that it goes away but that they are able to carry it day after day, push it along, drag it behind.

Enough time passed that the pain of losing my wife dulled and then went numb. The image of her with another man no longer makes me blind. In fact, I'm able to wish her well with her current man.

I've seen her a couple times in the five years since our breakup. Still in love with her. I suppose that's why I called it *Crazy Love*.

GETTING BETTER,
GENERATION BY GENERATION

A F T E R I got the job at the Foundation, I was able to move out of Josh's and Kathy's house and into an apartment. Then, with the Foundation's employer-assisted-housing program, I was able to buy a place of my own. When I moved to that townhouse in the Del Ray section of Alexandria, Virginia, I was putting my bed together, balancing the footboard to attach the side rails, when I noticed something sticking out from a wide board running the width of the footboard. I managed to get two fingers on it and twisted it back and forth until I pulled it out. It was a laminated identification card. My immediate assumption was that someone at the bed manufacturing plant had accidentally dropped his or her ID. I turned it over to see what name was on it. More than a name, there's a photograph on this laminated ID card. It was my father, dead these many years.

I remember that moment with exquisite precision, exactly where I was standing, exactly how I was holding the card, exactly my level of disbelief and utter bewilderment. How the hell did my dad's ID card get wedged into my bed, which I had purchased just the year before, many years after his death.

I stepped to a window to get some air. Had the old man gotten a job at a furniture manufacturer? I began considering the possibility of a ghost, of a haunting. I was unable to fill in the blanks with even the most outlandish possibilities. I simply could not figure it out.

Then I did. Several months before, I had traveled to Illinois to help my sister Nancy and my brother, Eric, close down my mother's house because she had moved into a nursing home. (My sister Linda had died some years before this—missed then and missed ever since.) Beyond a few items that came with dangling memories, my mother's things held no love or affection for us, so basically we cleaned out the house to get it ready for sale and put all her stuff on folding tables to sell to the good country folk who didn't have quite enough of their own junk in their lives and might want some of my mother's. My sister and brother and I gave each other permission to take a few things as mementos. I threw my father's ID card into one of my suitcases and, when I got home, I upended the suitcase on my bed to sort through things. At that time, the card must've slid off the end of the mattress and landed in the space between the trim board and foot-board. Nothing but coincidence. At the time of the card's discovery, however, I thought the old man was still reaching for me.

When my father was dying at age fifty-nine, I stayed with him in the hospital.

"You gotta come in here," he called from the bathroom.

I went in. He was standing at the toilet. "You gotta wipe my butt. I can't."

His hand had been amputated.

I wiped his butt and said, "Dad."

I left home as soon as I could, age eighteen. Before then I had run away from home on occasion, always to get the snot beat out of me when someone finally returned me to him. But good God, look what had become of the man.

"Do you remember all the times I ran away from home?" I asked.

"Yeah, you never got far. What that tells me, you weren't serious about it."

"Jesus, you're a hard case."

"Your running away upset your sisters more than it did me."

My sister Nancy remembers one time when I was running away and, before I left, I asked her if she wanted anything on the off chance that I was captured once again and brought home. She said she wanted Blue Sputnik Bubble Gum. I got on my bicycle and rode to town, waiting at an intersection where I thought the Greyhound bus made its stop. But the bus never came for me and, that night, a neighbor saw me riding my bike on a highway after dark and without offering any options put the bike in the back of his truck and drove me home. The old man knocked me to the kitchen floor and waited wordlessly for me to stand, then knocked me down again. Nancy and Linda were upstairs crying softly, stuffing little corners of their blankets in their mouths so the old man wouldn't hear them. When I finally came upstairs, I stopped by and dropped something on Nancy's bed. She says that ever since then I've been her hero—purchased for the price of Blue Sputnik Bubble Gum. At the end of his life, the old man was diabetic and bullheaded about taking care of himself, and here he was dying at an age younger than I am now.

In the hospital, he told me, "You don't think I remember or care or that it had any effect on me."

I asked him what he was talking about.

"All that shit I did to you. The times I hit you. I remember. I remember all of them. I got something to ask you."

"Okay."

"I'm asking you now if you have it in your heart to forgive me."

I thought about it, then told him I couldn't. I told him I didn't have the authority to forgive him. I said, "Who I am today, you haven't done anything to me, this adult standing here, there's nothing to forgive. You need forgiveness from that eight-year-old boy you hauled off and knocked to the ground, kicked with your boots, hit with a board. He's not around to forgive you and I don't have the power to forgive you on his behalf."

"Talk about a hard case," he said. All the same, he said he was glad I'd given him an honest answer and not just *said* I forgave him. I could see he was calculating. "You know I'm dying. You're refusing to forgive an old man who's dying."

"Not so old," I reminded him. "You're fifty-nine."

"Still dying," he said.

That's the way we left it. Without emotion, no wavering voice, certainly no tears or embraces. The old man was tougher than a cob, he was a Marine.

Here's what I give him: my father did a better—kinder, more loving and thoughtful—job of raising me than his father did raising him. And I did better with my sons than my father did with me. I expect my sons, with their children, will do a vastly better job than I did with them. By the time their children get around to raising *their* children, we should be approaching perfection.

The world was different back in the day. People did things routinely that would have them arrested today. Once, when I was six years old, the old man asked me if I wanted to see smoke come out of his eyes. Sure I did. He inhaled a Chesterfield, held the smoke, and told me to watch his eyes carefully. As I was distracted by carefully watching his eyes, he slowly brought the tip of his cigarette toward my arm, eventually touching the inside of my wrist, making me jump and yelp. At which point the old man asked in fake sincerity, "Did you see the smoke come out of my eyes—it happened right when you jumped. Did you see it?" I shook my head and rubbed the inside of my wrist, unsure of what had just happened. I had the burn scar for years.

Another time, for another joke, he told me to pee on an electric fence we had just strung around a pig pen. I was too young to figure out that the electric charge would travel up the stream of urine, through my dick, up the urethra, and into my bladder. Tiny amperage but a thousand volts. It doubled me over and dropped me to my knees, making the old man laugh his ass off.

If someone did things like that to a child today, you and I would be outraged. But I don't feel outraged that it happened to me. Those were just part of a tough life. Taught me to be wary. And I'm not even sure we are qualified to judge the past.

While the old man was a throwback on many issues, on one important matter he was progressive. He wasn't infected with the poor white man's disease: bigotry. I'm not sure how he escaped it. Maybe through his wide reading and intelligence. Since you are probably not of the poor, working class, I should explain the infection. Poor people are natural allies. If we banded together and worked to better our lot in life, by sheer number we could stand up to the money class, the power brokers. Realizing the terrifying potential of the united multitudes, those in power set out to fragment poor and working people to ensure they can never reach their potential. One of the most powerful fragmentation forces available is racial bigotry.

In colonial days, the lives of white indentured servants and African slaves were similar in unrelenting labor and hopelessness—with of course two obvious differences. The white indentured servant could escape and, as a fugitive, take up a new life elsewhere in the colonies—an option that was not open to the black slave. And that slave had been taken from his home by force while the white servant signed up for his indentured service, although you could argue that the grinding poverty of the underclass robbed this indentured servitude of any real *choice*.

Seeing that these two groups—white indentured servants and black African slaves—were natural allies who spent time together and would have freely intermarried, the power class enforced a series of laws and social practices to break the alliance. White indentured servants were made overseers of slaves. Miscegenation laws were passed and severely enforced. Social practices, such as a slave stepping off a walkway to let pass a person of social standing, were enforced against black people, but not white people, even if the two were equally poor and bound to lifelong servitude.

It worked. Poor white people became infected with the idea that no matter how bad off you are, how poor, how lacking in dignity and opportunity—at least you're better than a nigger. The black man wants your job. And your woman. Keep them down. Don't associate with them.

I grew up in the coal-mining regions of Southern Illinois where, in 1898, before unions were legal, miners went on strike in Virden, Illinois. The mine owners sent a train into the Deep South to pick up poor blacks with the promise of good jobs up north. The owners could have found scab labor a lot closer to Virden but that labor would have been white. Bringing in black workers accomplished two goals, breaking the strike and showing white workers that everything they'd heard about black workers taking your jobs was true—here comes a trainload of them.

The workers fired on the train and company goons fired back. Seven miners were killed. In that area of Southern Illinois, no cemetery would permit burials of members of these illegal unions—until my hometown of Mount Olive opened Union Miners' Cemetery and allowed the victims of the Virden mine riot to be buried there. Mother Jones, the famous workers' rights advocate, came to Mount Olive at the dedication of the Virden Mine Riot Memorial and said that when she died she wanted to be buried right there, next to her boys. Her memorial has been restored now, but when I was in high school it was overgrown and neglected.

When I was growing up, the prejudice infection was endemic among poor working whites. Working in the steel mills, I heard it all the time—nigger this and nigger that. To fix something haphazardly was to nigger-rig it. To wrap a couple twenties around a fat roll of singles to make it seem you were in possession of serious money instead of just that pocketful of ones—that was called a nigger roll. Borrow a drag off someone's cigarette and hand it back with a wet tip and you were accused of nigger lipping. Eenie, meenie, miney, moe, catch a nigger by the toe . . . My father's parents casually referred to brazil nuts as nigger toes and black children as pickaninnies, and my grandfather would open a newspaper with a comment, "Wonder what the niggers want today?"

For whatever reason, my father, however, was totally, beautifully clean of this infection. I never heard him say nigger in my entire life and if I had used the word in his presence he would've knocked me to the ground. He had black friends, which was scandalous in that day. If his white friends or coworkers were over at our house and said something about niggers this, niggers that—the old man would tell the person that such talk was ignorant. If the person repeated it, the old man would stand up and tell him, "Get the fuck out of my house."

So of all the burdens a poor person has to overcome to make it into the middle class, I was at least free of the infection. Thanks to the old man. He allowed me to jump ahead a generation. This gave my sons a head start, too.

I wasn't smart about money, but I made a canny investment in sons. I would not have made it through losing everything without Matt and Josh and my daughter-in-law, Kathy. Matt married Amanda last year, and now there are four of them, smart and articulate and brilliant to be around. In many ways, I have at long last become what my first wife wanted me to be during our marriage: a family man. The rage to live and write and drink that made me crazy and ambitious, desperate and arrogant, horny and dangerous—if that rage has not burned out, at least it's banked. And now, holding my granddaughter on my lap is enough. Sometimes when I'm driving up to their house to see her after a week's absence, I find myself smiling in anticipation.

8

TRYING TO GET SMARTER

IN THIS new period of domestication, I'm trying to be smarter about things, trying to see situations from the perspective of others. When my ex-wife said the affair she had was not about me but was about what *she* was going through in her life, I was incredulous. Her affair had *everything* to do with me. It changed my life, made me go crazy. She said going crazy was *my* doing, not hers. And she insisted that the affair had to do with where she was in her life, sorting out getting older, gauging whether she was still attractive, seeing if romance was still possible. It was about her, not me.

Another thing she told me that eventually made sense came in response to my assertion, made after the worst of the anguish was over, that she should cut me some slack because although I went crazy during that summer, for eighteen years I had been calm, reasonable, loving, and emotionally secure. My argument was that one episode of madness should be judged within the context of eighteen years of reasonableness. Her counterpoint, which I didn't appreciate until later, was that the unprecedented nature of my insanity made it *more* frightening. If I had gone wacko on several occasions before all this, she could have put my over-the-edge behavior within context—he always was a little crazy. But because I had never gone crazy before, she had no perspective on what caused it or when it might come again.

Of all the post-breakup analyses she and I conducted together, the most serious indictment of me came when she said I wanted it to happen. I rejected this at first, too. How could I have *wanted* her to betray me, how could I have *wanted* to lose my mind. But she meant I wanted the breakup of our marriage. She reminded me that I have always said I dreamed of being free of encumbrances, that my life's ambition was to be alone in a room with nothing to do but write. Maybe, she said, I saw *her* affair as *my* way out of the marriage. I could get a divorce and yet be blameless because I hadn't done anything, *she* had. When I discovered her affair, it had not yet been consummated, was more silly than serious, was not a threat to our marriage. I made it a threat. I escalated everything. I made this the most serious thing that had ever happened to us. Having successfully inflated it to a massive size, I then declared it too heavy to bear and divorced her.

What if it's true? I always tell people that for the most part we arrange our lives to get what we want. That if we oversleep and miss a flight, it's probably because we truly did not want to make that trip.

It's a hell of a thing if I subconsciously created the breakup of our marriage when in fact we could have stayed together.

We don't think about our lives. We don't analyze. We don't examine. We go through our lives, day after day, one row at a time, without ever pausing long enough to speculate. Why don't we ask ourselves, why am I working at this job? Why am I with this man, this woman? Why do I live where I live?

Asking these Big Questions is considered adolescent. Answers to these questions are supposedly obvious. I'm working here because I need the money. I'm living here because this is near where I work.

But that's not answering the Big Questions, that's avoiding them. If you're willing to entertain big-and-adolescent questions, your life examinations will lead you to think about—and to consider *making*— life changes. And changing our lives is a potential danger and *that's* the reason we go day after day without looking too closely at what we do and why we do it—we don't want to put the status quo at risk.

So what we do is, we discipline the Guys in the Back Row until they know their places. We yell at them to shut up and we never allow them to stand and speak their piece and we constantly let them know how ashamed we are of their unruly, unrealistic, flighty selves—until finally they are cowed and no longer a threat. When we accomplish that, when we have brought the Guys in the Back Row to heel, then we'll have our lives under control. And the Guys in the Back Row with their memories and urges and what-ifs won't bother us anymore. Walking along a lake on a summer's day, we won't ponder so deeply it hurts how life might've been had we stayed with that person who loved us madly, truly. Watching children, we won't regret to the point of tears our decision to have them or not to have them. The External Reality Team is doing its job as efficiently as ever, regular contributions to our 401(k) keep getting made, promotions are deftly earned, pills smooth moods, and fears don't nudge us awake at 3 a.m. The world says we are a success! But what might happen, long after we have disciplined and controlled and lobotomized the Guys in the Back Row into no longer being a danger to the deportment of our orderly lives . . . we might discover we are alone. Where is the poet who once lived in our head? Where is that adventurer, the explorer? The mountaineer, the musician, the risk taker? The sailor? The teacher? Actor? Storyteller? Lover? The one who weeps at movies about dogs in danger and children who never fit in and then do at long last, to swelling music, fit in? We call on the Guys in the Back Row, request an old song, ask for a story, a memory, something to make us feel something, please, God, let me feel *something* one more time. Ah. Those you call on sit still in the Back Row of your mind. But you have so successfully forced them into shamed silence for so long that now they stare blankly, nothing left, no longer a threat, and no longer part of us, leaving us bereft and leaving us utterly alone in the world.

A friend told me about going to a top executive's retirement party, a guy who had left his job a millionaire many times over. My friend reminded the retiring executive of a conversation that the two of them had had twenty years before, when they were idealists vowing to leave the world a better place than they'd found it. But instead of pursuing his ideals, the retiring executive learned to march lockstep with corporate doctrine, get promoted and receive fat bonuses and increase his retirement accounts. My friend asked the executive how he made peace with having abandoned his idealism, and the retiring executive, in his cups, admitted that voices spoke to him of that idealism for many years. But eventually he quieted them by killing them. That's how he shut up his Guys in the Back Row.

Although I've become domesticated, my Guys in the Back Row have stayed alive, shouting their advice, offering running commentaries on how the External Reality Team is ruining things by being uptight jerks who never saw an ass they wouldn't kiss. If you think I'm bragging about keeping my Guys in the Back Row alive and active, that I'm smug about it, you'd be wrong. This decision in favor of the Guys in the Back Row has been a burden in a variety of ways. Mostly financial.

You must be weary by now of my references to money. But if you read an artist's memoirs in which money—getting it, losing it, worrying about it—is *not* a major theme, I can promise you that the writer/painter/playwright/poet you are reading about was never poor. Was not born poor, did not live poor. Because if you don't have money, then no matter how devoted you are to your art, you will dwell on money. You never have the luxury of saying, as well-off artists are always finding opportunities to say, *I'm doing it for the art, not the money*. Well, I'm so happy for you, you rich asshole. Try being poor. In-debt poor. Poor in your brain even when there's money in your bank.

Many people my age who stayed in good jobs and kept their noses clean and their Guys in the Back Row quiet are now well off, work in big corner offices, go home to spectacular houses and smiling spouses. What they worry about, they tell me in all sincerity, is how they are going to *wisely* spend their fortunes. To enrich their children and grandchildren, of course—but in ways that don't rob those generations of opportunities to succeed on their own.

I have been known to spill wine to derail these conversations. Because my worries are different. I worry that if I quit work, how am I going to pay for medicine and, in those months when I can't afford the pills, what will the diabetes do to my body, and will I end up like my father and his parents, losing a hand, losing a foot, losing a leg. I worry if I'll have a place to live. I worry about showing up on my sons' doorsteps *a second time*. I worry if I die alone, how long will it take for someone to find the body.

So if I worry about these things, why don't I keep the safe and good-paying and nicely benefited job I now have?

The Guys in the Back Row want to answer that:

Because we are a fucking novelist, that's why, asshole!

They've always had issues with impulse control.

We're quitting work because no fucking way are we living the rest of our life making stupid little quips about Thank God It's Friday and Oh, No, Another Monday.

I try to tell them the job is not that bad, let's hold on for a few more years. But they won't listen to this good advice, and they're always making trouble for me.

I was talking with a woman at work who said, while making photocopies near my wee little cubicle, "Here it is Friday and it seems like just yesterday that I came over here and was saying to you here it is Monday again." I agreed with her that time flies. But she said she *likes* the fact that time flies by when she's busy. "Here a whole week has gone by and it seemed like only a couple days."

Yes, I said, weeks fly by and the summer's gone when it seems like spring was just here and then the years go flying by and you wonder where all the time went, you wonder how it was that you managed to get old, then you retire and those retirement years whip by in an instant and then as you're dying you can think, Wow, that went by so quickly!

Now she doesn't talk to me when she comes near my cubicle to make photocopies. My Guys in the Back Row weren't nice to her.

They're not nice to anyone. When I ride up in the elevator on a Monday morning and two people are discussing their weekend, the Guys in the Back Row goad me into making faces that mock what the others are saying.

"How was your weekend?" one elevator rider asked his coworker.

"Too short!" the other exclaimed—actually exclaimed.

"*Too short!*" Ha-ha-ha-ha-ha-ha! "Aren't they *all* short?"

"Yes, *all* of them!" Ha-ha-ha-ha-ha-ha-ha.

"Weekends *zoom* by!" Ha-ha-ha-ha-ha-ha-ha-ha!

"Zoom by!" Ha-ha-ha-ha-ha-ha-ha!

And if they see me making faces that mock their conversation, how long will it be before I have to leave? Ha-ha.

I've worked in offices about twenty-five years of my life but never more than three years at a time. I've always been successful in these jobs but at some point the Guys in the Back Row just can't take it anymore and keep insisting, *I thought we were a writer.*

So I throw myself into new life adventures . . . fall down seven times, get up eight. I fall down by myself but always get up with someone's help.

When I was in the middle of my suicidal anguish, under threat of a lawsuit that would take my copyrights, my life's work, being cuckolded and lied to, sick with uncontrolled glucose . . . I told David Rosenthal of Simon & Schuster that I needed a book contract. I hadn't hit bottom yet—that was to come in an emergency room some months later—but I was close. I needed to know I would have at least one more book published before I died. Having lost everything, I needed one last time to be a writer. Rosenthal said yes and gave me a small contract that was large enough to save my life.

When I was down and out, I had friends who said I should name what I needed and they would send it. I've known Johanna Crighton for twenty-five years but we haven't seen each other for half that time because she lives in England. She kept e-mailing me, asking why I wasn't e-mailing her back. When I was finally able to tell her I had hit bottom, she asked me how much money would put me back on my feet because she would send it right away. There was never any doubt in my mind that her offer was immediately available. Johanna came to visit me after I got back on my feet and we became friends all over again.

Jon and Myra Carlock told me repeatedly that all I had to do was call them and they would put me up for as long as I needed a home. I never took anyone up on these offers but having friends like these has to be better than having money in the bank—because you can spend the money and then it's gone but you can draw on the friendships for the rest of your life.

I also came across strangers who turned out to be angels. When the Hollywood person was calling me weekly, threatening to take everything, I couldn't find a lawyer to represent me because I didn't have the money for a retainer. I made dozens of calls and sent dozens of e-mails and actually visited a few lawyers. Most were sympathetic but they weren't going to take my case for free. And then I called an attorney who had a blog online and when I got through to him, the first thing he asked me wasn't about the case but about the books I've written. He loved books and writers and took my case because it was the right thing to do, by his way of thinking. This was not a matter of working on a contingency. There was no settlement to win. My goal was simply to make this Hollywood person leave me alone. This heroic lawyer (yes! you can use those two words in conjunction), who didn't know me, whom I have never met, said I could pay him when I was back on my feet. He got the producer to back off. I'm not mentioning this lawyer's name because I haven't been able to contact him. I've sent letters and e-mails saying that I now have a job, I've saved some money, I calculated the hours he probably spent on this case, and I'm ready to send him a check. But I've never heard back.

Meeting him was a grace. So is my family. So are my friends. I have friends who've been long-term investments, like Barbara Parker, a friend for thirty years. I've also made brand-new investments, like a friend I met just a few years ago, who suffers from depression and knows what it feels like in the middle of the night when 3 a.m. weighs too much to carry alone. These graces are the investments I have instead of a retirement fund. They are accounts I draw from to stay alive.

9

LEARNING TO BLESS MY ENEMIES

FACING RUSHMORE, my eleventh novel, was published in 2005. It's about the ultimate revenge of American Indians, victims of the longest sustained genocide in history. Through *Facing Rushmore*, I met Jay Winter Nightwolf, an Indian activist, spokesman, and radio personality. And from Jay I learned a different kind of wisdom.

He told me that two wolves were battling for control of my life. One wolf, Jay said, represented everything that was good about me. Generosity. A willingness to forgive. A deep commitment to being an honorable man and doing the right thing. All the aspects of my life that would make me proud of myself.

The other wolf battling for control of my life represents everything about myself that I'm ashamed of. The resentment I feel when someone else succeeds. The arrogance of thinking I know what's best for other people. Any wish I've ever had for something bad to happen to someone who's done me wrong. The greed I feel in longing for commercial success.

Jay had described both of my wolves with amazing accuracy. Furthermore, he said, the two wolves were battling each other right now to define my life. "And, David, I know which one wins."

"You do?"

"Yes."

"Which one?"

"The one you feed, David. That's the one who wins."

To ensure that the wolf fighting on behalf of my good instincts would win over the wolf representing everything craven about me, Jay explained ways I could feed the good wolf. He told me of something his grandmother had taught him. Each time she crossed water (a lake, pond, river, inlet), she said a conscious and sincere prayer, asking that her enemies be blessed and that they prosper. Each time she crossed water and made this prayer on behalf of an enemy, she had a specific person in mind. She would figuratively throw the blessing into the water, and it would float away, carrying with it the bitterness she held in her heart toward that enemy. Blessing her enemies fed the good wolf within her, strengthening it to win the battle and freeing her soul of the bad karma we accumulate by wishing ill to others.

I lived in Virginia and worked in the District so I had opportunities twice a day, coming and going to the office, to bless my enemies and send that blessing and my bitterness into the Potomac River. I did this blithely, I'm afraid—not truly honoring Jay's grandmother. If someone said something sharp to me at work, I would bless this "enemy" as I crossed the Potomac that evening. If someone in traffic gave me the finger, I would bless him as I crossed the Potomac next morning. Trivial stuff.

Waiting to merge onto Rock Creek Parkway one day, I accidentally bumped into the back of a car that had started to merge, then stopped. No damage done to either vehicle, but the driver of the other car was *livid*. She had short white hair and spoke (screeched) with a heavy German accent. I apologized for bumping into her and she apparently took this as an invitation to rip into me. I was an idiot. Where did I learn to drive? She couldn't believe the idiots who are on the road today. If I had caused damage she would've lost work taking care of the repairs. On and on. Screaming at me. I finally asked what she wanted from me—there was no damage and I had already apologized. Apparently what she wanted was for me to stand there so she could continue ripping into me. This awful little white-haired German woman finally got into her car and rushed into traffic, almost hitting a car. Next time I crossed the Potomac, I blessed her and wished for her to achieve serenity in her life.

But as I was blessing the crazy German woman, it finally occurred to me I was trivializing the wise counsel from Jay's grandmother. The people I had been blessing were not my enemies. I had two enemies, two individuals whose actions had contributed to the ruin of my life. I could debate the *size* of their contributions, as compared to my own responsibility for running through a fortune, not paying attention to my career, slacking off, not taking action until too late to correct my mistakes. But what I did to myself, I did to myself. What they did to me was an entirely different manner. One of them had threatened financial ruin, the other had used friendship to engineer his affair with my wife. They had wronged me. They were enemies.

Could I cross the Potomac River and bless them? Could I sincerely hope that they prospered and were happy? If I could, then I was being serious about the healing that Jay's grandmother's intended. If I couldn't, then I should stop pretending to bless people as I crossed the river because I was just fooling around.

I remember the particular afternoon when I first tried to be serious about this, driving across the Key Bridge from the District to Virginia, looking down at the Potomac River and thinking—I'm going to sincerely, earnestly, honestly bless my wife's boyfriend and hope that he prospers in his life and finds happiness and peace. This was one of the most difficult internal struggles I've ever undertaken. The exercise was meaningless unless I meant it. As I crossed the waters of the Potomac, I spoke aloud: "I bless [his name] and hope that he prospers and achieves happiness in his life." And I meant it. Then I dedicated this blessing to the waters of the Potomac and let the river carry away my blessing along with the bitterness in my heart.

The idea was not to forgive him. Or to forget what he had done. The idea was to send away whatever connection that still tied me to him.

It didn't work in one shot. There was so much bitterness in my heart that the amount I was able to throw in the river this first time didn't get rid of it all.

So I blessed him again while crossing back over the river and hoped once again that he prospered—and once again I meant it sincerely. I added to my blessing. I hope your marriage is happy. I hope your wife has forgiven you. I hope your son prospers. And with that, a little more of my bitterness went into the river along with my blessing. Hell, by the time I got rid of the bitterness in my heart for this guy, I bet he had received more blessings from me than he'd ever gotten from his dear old mom. If wishing someone well counts for anything, by now this guy must be one prosperous asshole.

I did the same thing for the other person, the Hollywood person. And for him, my blessings must've worked because he went from obscurity to being connected with some gigantic movies. And he will never know that he has me to thank.

As I continued doing this, sincerely blessing my enemies, the very act of doing it became easier. I could feel that the rock I had been carrying in my heart was becoming smaller, its edges smoother. I even began to understand my enemies' perspective. The Hollywood person truly believed that he had been betrayed by me and others he'd worked with. He thought I was lying when I told him what really happened. And the guy in Tennessee didn't rape my wife, he seduced her—or was seduced by her. And his efforts to befriend me to throw me off the track—actually, it's a pretty good strategy when you think about it. Lies have to be told to support an adulterous affair. The only thing the guy should not have done was laugh at me. Still some bitterness was left about that. I'm working on it, still throwing stuff overboard each time I cross water.

One day walking in a park with a friend, we went over a wooden footbridge and I told her about blessing your enemies when crossing water. Her initial reaction was like mine had been, lighthearted as she forgave someone who spilled a latte on her that morning. I had to explain. It's not about forgiving someone. And it's not meant for someone who caused a minor irritation. It's about summoning the goodwill within you to actually bless an enemy, to actually wish that the person who has done you wrong will prosper and find happiness. It ennobles *you* and feeds the right wolf.

In that case, she said, if we're being serious about this, she didn't have any real enemies.

Ah, that's what many people say. But there's always someone.

I mentioned the name of someone who had betrayed her in a business setting. The woman who had committed the betrayal went on to become very successful. The betrayal ate at my friend, and when I suggested that this other woman was the person she should bless and offer good wishes to, whether or not you call her an enemy— my friend hesitated. That's when I knew we were on to something. If you hesitate in blessing a person, that's the person you need to bless. My friend said that this other person, her supposed enemy—already has success. I said, then you should hope and pray she has even more success. If she has won one award, undeserved or not, you should wish she wins three more. And if she and her husband make a combined income of $3 million a year, you should send her a blessing that their income doubles to $6 million. And you have to mean the blessing, you can't just say it.

"And then when you've made that sincere blessing and have hoped for her prosperity," I told my friend, "you drop the blessings into the creek and they will float away carrying with them the rancor you still feel toward this woman."

This galled my friend but she did it. Or said she did it. I wasn't sure. She sometimes goes along with my suggestions just to shut me up.

But a few weeks later she told me she had continued to bless this woman and send her best wishes each time she crossed a body of water, and she was beginning to feel that the hold the other woman had over her—causing her to experience hateful feelings—was getting weaker and weaker.

Try it. Use the crossing of a body of water as your reminder. If you do it enough, the very sight of water below you will trigger a reminder. Think of someone who has done you wrong, betrayed you, lied about you, left you. Wish good things for that person. Hope that the person prospers financially and stays healthy and finds true love and serenity.

Mean it. And then send the blessing and your bitterness into the water to be carried away.

Someone asked me if I blessed my ex-wife whenever I crossed a river. It had never occurred to me. I didn't consider her an enemy. I've *always* wanted her to prosper and stay healthy and be happy—I didn't need to cross water to wish for that. Why would you wish for anything but the best for someone you've loved since the beginning of time?

2 0

LESSONS

I WOULD NOT have written this book as just another entry in the sweepstakes of memoirs that shock us readers with accounts of depravity and drugs, horrible childhoods, and terrible losses. My story would not have won any prizes in that sweepstakes because other people have suffered more, done worse, overcome higher obstacles. I've talked with a lot of people who've lost a lot in their lives, and many of those accounts are more harrowing than anything in these pages. When we lived in Saratoga Springs, we met an older couple who owned a few apartment buildings and seemed in every sense normal, successful, well adjusted. I used to argue with the guy about politics. One evening when they were over at our house, I noticed numbers tattooed on his forearm. Compared to him and so many others I have talked with, I didn't really lose everything—I just got knocked on my ass and took a while to stand up again.

In the course of getting back on my feet and talking with people who've lost everything and bounced back, I've learned some lessons.

Cultivate a habit of asking why. I worked for a woman who has a habit—regarding both work issues and personal matters—of asking why. If I brought in an assignment, a message to employees about an upcoming project, for example, and if I had written the copy with puns and humor instead of covering it seriously, she would ask why. Not that she was against the style of humor, but she wanted to know if I was aware of and could explain why I chose it. And then when we became friends outside of that office setting and I told her I had decided to do something, to send my ex-wife a CD, for example, or accept a weekend trip invitation from someone I had just met—my friend would ask why had I made those decisions. You'd be surprised how many times you do something, often something significant, without ever asking yourself why you were doing it. If you follow my friend's advice and develop a habit of asking why, you'll gain an element of knowledge about, if not control over, your life.

Never lose a sense of wonderment. I grew up amid small-town Midwest smugness that wouldn't permit people to be impressed, be wowed, be amazed. I think Midwesterners developed this attitude to protect against being flimflammed. They were isolated and insular and therefore vulnerable. As protection against snake oil salesmen and rainmakers and politicians and others who promised magic, the Midwesterners learned to shrug. This might provide immunity from scams but it's no way to go through life, being profoundly unimpressed. When I was a boy I watched The Ed Sullivan Show with a group of family and neighbors. One of the performers spun plates on flexible sticks. He got several plates spinning on those sticks. He then put the sticks in holes on a table, the plates still spinning. He picked up more sticks and plates and got them spinning. By this time, the original spinning plates were slowing down, wobbling, threatening to fall off their sticks, and he would rush back to them and get them spinning again, start several new plates spinning, taking care of others that had slowed down, and more, wobbling, almost falling off their sticks. I was amazed. How many plates could this madman keep spinning? How many more could he possibly add to the already unbelievable number he had spinning? He's astonishing, he's—and just as I'm ready to stand and cheer, here comes the smug disbelief.

He's cheating, someone in the room said.

Others eagerly agreed. "Those plates are connected to those sticks, they ain't going to fall."

"What they're not showing you, when the camera is on him, is that someone sneaks in and keeps them other plates spinning."

"They use mirrors and camera tricks, everybody knows that."

So there I sat in absolute wonderment, wanting to cheer the madman spinning plates, while all around me relatives and neighbors were dismissive and unimpressed and contemptuous. Even back then I thought, I gotta get out of here. I sometimes notice this same Midwestern lack of wonderment among sophisticated people who apparently consider enthusiasm to be gauche. I'm happy to report that I remain as gauche as I can possibly be, discovering amazements on a daily basis. String theory and quantum physics are wonderments even if they threaten to make my head explode. I'll read a sentence from a Truman Capote essay and decide it's among the most beautiful sentences I've ever read in my life. I'll look across the room at a woman and conclude that she is the most wonderful thing I will ever see. The other night I thought the house up the road was on fire, because I saw something red shimmering through the trees. Before driving there to find out what was happening, I looked through binoculars. It was the moon. Rising as red as the sun through the trees. It was astonishing. It gave me a reason to be happy I was alive. I wanted to call everyone I knew to tell them about this moon as red as blood. These kinds of enthusiasms make me a goofball but I hold the same hope for you, that you never lose the ability to be impressed.

Be comforted by the fact that what you've gone through in losing everything will give you a baseline against which you can compare all

other calamities in your life. This was told to me by someone who lost
a true love who had come late into her life; having his death occur so
soon after they met caused her to collapse so profoundly that she very
nearly never recovered. But she did. And as she rebuilt her life and
then the usual disasters in business occurred, she said she was always
able to put those disappointments into perspective against losing him,
against a time in her life, an experience in her life, that she knew was
truly as bad as it could ever get for her. I sometimes forget this. I am a
drama king so when something goes wrong in my life I immediately
start clearing my throat in preparation of great lamentations. I'm grateful, therefore, for this woman's reminder that nothing now is going to
be as bad as ending up on the floor in Tennessee insane.

And when things do get really bad, remember: At least you don't
own a monkey. The old man would say this occasionally when events
went poorly for us. The first time I remember hearing it, we had a flat
on a country road on our way to someone's house. I got out of the car
with the old man and as soon as I saw the flat, I quickly looked at him
to see if we would be visited by the rage or not. For some reason, this
particular evening, not. Instead, the old man turned to me and said
softly, "At least we don't own a monkey." I was never sure what he
meant by that, if it was an old saying or if he meant it literally—because he had a cousin who did own a monkey that was the meanest,
dirtiest creature I've ever encountered. An entire sunroom attached to
the cousin's house was given over to this monkey, and you entered
that room at your own peril. Owning a monkey is a terrible thing for
the monkey and no picnic for the owners either.

It was in the monkey's sunroom that I saw my first pornographic
picture. My father's cousin's son had a deck of naughty playing cards.
He agreed to show me just one. I remember it. The queen of diamonds was a color photograph of a woman wearing no clothes. I was
more amazed by this than I was by the monkey.

I remember her precisely. She had large breasts, you won't be surprised to hear. She was sitting on the floor with her legs widely spread

and the soles of her feet touching in front of her. A crystal bowl sat on the floor at the juncture of her legs. She had both hands on that bowl. Her expression was kindly as if to say, *Please, young Master Martin, go ahead and look at my breasts, I do not mind.* I'm not sure why she would talk stilted like that. Her hair was swept up off her neck and was pinned on top of her head. I was at that worst possible adolescent age where a picture like that could change my life.

I wanted a few more precious moments to *look* at the picture but that fucking monkey started throwing his feces, and the plastic-coated playing card was snatched from my hand as I and my father's cousin's son beat a hasty retreat under a hail of monkey shit.

My point is . . . actually I just wanted to tell you the monkey story. But sometimes we punish ourselves when it's unnecessary, when in fact our situation is not that bad, when we forget the ongoing blessing of not owning a monkey. I had a friend who told me that her greatest fear in life was being forced to drive a city bus. She knew she wouldn't be able to steer properly. She wouldn't be able to maneuver in traffic without hitting cars and pedestrians. Wouldn't know which stops she should make. I pointed out that while being forced to drive a bus might be frightening, the chances of it ever actually occurring were infinitesimally small. Which gave her little comfort, such was her fear. So I'm trying to take my own advice and ease up, back off, calm down. I will not be forced against my will to drive a city bus and no matter how bad I think things are, I can rejoice in the knowledge that at least I don't own a monkey.

Learning is hard, but harder still is unlearning. In the months I was recovering from losing everything, my daughter-in-law, Kathy, was a rock. She never let me get away with anything and insisted on knowing why I had begun to hate women.

I don't hate women! I love women. Kathy said it didn't sound like I loved women, not from the things I was saying. Like what? Like jokes about women being easy, like snide comments about women acting like sluts. Did I really say those things? Did I believe them?

Had I started to hate women because of my wife's infidelity? I never cheated on her in eighteen years. Did I believe my fidelity gave me a crown of superiority, the right to criticize and belittle and *hate* women?

I didn't *want* to hate women, and as Kathy kept calling me on it, I began a process of trying to unlearn what was already in my head. Which is when I discovered that unlearning is more difficult than learning. First step in my unlearning was to stop saying it. Even if a joke about a woman cheating on her husband came into my head, I would not give voice to it. Even if someone who didn't know better asked where my wife was and what was she doing and that question gave me a perfect opportunity to say something witty and rude about where she was and who she was with, I no longer took that opportunity to voice those thoughts even as I continued to think them.

This first step, of no longer saying it, has an amazing effect: eventually you stop thinking it.

More often than you think, we choose exactly the kind of life we're living. This is a hard pill for a lot of us to choke down, because we are absolutely convinced we did NOT WANT to end up working in a corporation; we wanted to be a jazz musician or actress or work with big cats in the zoo. We did NOT WANT the kind of marriage we now have. But in fact we choose to work where we work and we choose to be married to whom we are married.

To put it another way, we are unwilling to pay the price required to get us out of our current career or marriage or whatever else it is we feel trapped in. I learned this lesson through something I mentioned earlier, my ex-wife's assertion that maybe I wanted to be out of our marriage and that's why I made her fling so devastating that our marriage wouldn't recover from it. What she says makes a lot of sense.

I have a friend who's had a lifelong pattern of ruining his chances for success when he's right at the moment of achieving that success. This is not my assessment, it's his. He was chosen to be a Rhodes scholar; that would have put him in the same year class with Bill Clinton and might well have changed the trajectory of my friend's entire life. Just weeks before he was to leave for England, he got married. When he told this to his advisor, the guy was appalled. Did my friend realize that (at the time) Rhodes scholars could not be married and that this marriage now disqualified him? My friend says he didn't realize it, what dumb luck, how stupid of him. But at some level he must have known that a major event like marriage might have an effect on this scholarship—yet he went ahead and let it unspool.

This is one of half a dozen similar events. He poisoned a relationship with his PhD advisor right before the guy was to make recommendations for my friend to get a teaching position. My friend sent a wildly inappropriate e-mail to the entire staff where he worked right before decisions were made about who would be laid off and who would continue having a job. I would argue that my friend chose not to have a Rhodes Scholarship, chose not to get a good teaching job, chose not to continue in his job. Why, I have no idea.

When you do things or fail to do things that lead you to live your life in certain ways, I think you are making those choices either proactively or out of a fear of the alternatives. This is a good lesson to learn. Next time my friend is on the cusp of a major success in his life, he might benefit from considering whether he wants it or not, whether he's going to sabotage it or not. And if I had been presented with this lesson after discovering my wife's infidelity, I might have taken a longer, colder, harder look at my own actions and motivations in reacting so dramatically to her affair. This might be the hardest thing you ever learn to accept—that for the most part, we lead the lives we've chosen for ourselves.

Jump, skip, and take pleasure in small things. One day on the Internet I discovered a new typeface that I thought was delightful, especially the jaunty ampersand. When I rushed this discovery to a woman I worked with, she said it was good I could become so enthusiastic over a typeface and assured me, "As long as you can take pleasure in small things, you'll always have a chance at happiness." She was an older woman.

I love older women for their dry-eyed wisdom. Another older woman of my acquaintance once lamented to me that she had lost the ability to jump. I think she was eighty-three when we had this conversation, and she wondered if she had lost the ability to jump when she was in her late sixties or was it later, maybe she could still jump at age seventy-five. She said that if she had realized she was going to lose the ability to jump, she would've been tracking it all along so that she would know with more certainty when she could jump and when she could no longer jump. Now that I'm aware of this, I jump occasionally just to make sure I can still get both feet off the ground. Wait. I just got up from the computer and jumped. I can still jump.

One day at work I challenged my friends, Carl Luty and Kathy Litzenberg, to see if they could skip. You know, like when you were a kid. If you haven't skipped for many years, your first attempts are going to be hilarious, I guarantee you. But then you remember the rhythms and after a few goofy missteps, there you are—skipping again. You can't skip and not laugh, that's what we discovered. After our skipping up and down the hallways became distracting for our non-skipping colleagues, we took skipping to the underground parking lot where we skipped like nobody's business. Do you realize how much ground you can cover while skipping? It was goofy but brilliant, two men approaching sixty and a young woman, skipping through a parking garage. I think people should skip instead of jog. Joggers jog with faces grim while skippers skip with a grin.

I was walking along the beach with best friends and failed vineyard partners Ambrose Clancy and Mary Lydon, when I told them about skipping with Carl and Kathy. Mary wasn't sure she remembered how to skip but we held hands and took off and soon we were skipping like children down the beach—leaving behind Ambrose who was performing some kind of crippled hopping motion in the sand. Mary and I made the mistake of laughing at him and he stopped trying to skip. Ambrose, I urge you—please try again to skip. And, Mary, if he does—*please* videotape it.

I urge all of you to make sure you can still jump. Try to skip. And take pleasure where you find it, in even the smallest of ampersands.

Meet death like a warrior. This is something else I learned from Jay Winter Nightwolf. Don't meet death afraid, meet it like the warrior you are. All the trials you've faced in life, all the trails you've traveled, all the battles you've survived, all the things you've carried and pushed and pulled—these life struggles make you a warrior. Don't diminish that heroic life by being afraid at the end of it. I'm no longer that eight-year-old boy weeping in the bathtub at the knowledge and prospect of my own death. I don't fear being dead. But I am afraid of a bad death, a lingering death, a hospital-and-tube death. So I try to remember what Jay says: face death like a warrior and ask your family and friends to gather close and sing you home.

Beware the beast. I had no idea how hard life could be until the beast came for me—and you probably don't either. I'm not talking about being passed over for a promotion or being told you need an operation. I'm talking about a full-on brutalizing assault that continues for months or years, intending to humiliate you, kill you, break your heart. That truck drifting across the center line to kill your only child. The love of your life betraying you. Going bankrupt. Crippling depression. Cancer that ravages your body. Losing your mind. I wish I had known the beast's dimensions, I would not have been so arrogant, I would've prepared myself and then, when the beast arrived, I would've fought harder.

The people I talked with about losing everything used similar language when discussing the beast. A family friend, Hugh, was visited by a debilitating depression that he referred to as the black dog, which is the term Churchill used for his depression.

People told me they couldn't believe it was happening, weren't prepared for what came next, were astonished that a loved one or business partner was capable of doing/saying whatever she/he said or did.

Believe it.

If you think a beast doesn't exist for you, then put this book back where you found it and pray for mercy on your ignorant soul.

Never forget the sins you've committed. I should've known better than to go out into the woods with that boy a second time. He's the one who carried the water jug the last few steps of an arduous trip and got me slapped to the ground by my father, who thought I had let the boy carry the water the whole way. It was a tough lesson to learn at age eight, but I still admired the older boy—he owned a pocketknife. One day during that long summer when I was eight and we were putting up fence, he suggested to our fathers that we could go pick some blackberries and bring them back for all to share. I should've told him I would go my separate way and pick my own goddamn blackberries, you sly bastard. But I was eight, he was twelve, and he owned that damn wonderful pocketknife.

We came upon a toad.

I wrote a book, *Crazy Love*, that talked about the treatment of animals. I am not opposed to raising animals for food, butchering them, eating them. I have killed too many animals to tell about here. Not just the chickens and hogs we killed to butcher but also cats that had been left by the side of the road, too injured to live and in agony, dogs abandoned by their owners and starving to death, cows that were down with something and would never get up again. This might seem primitive to you, that I've killed so many animals, but I've always tried to treat animals in my care with dignity even as I was killing them. I cannot abide cruelty in any form to any animal. I have never been intentionally cruel to an animal.

Except for that poor, pitiful toad.

I believe that in the afterlife we atone for our treatment of animals, that we are honored for our kindnesses to animals and must explain our cruelties to them. I'm not sure how this works—since I don't know how the afterlife works, except as I understood it at the Broken Down Valise. But I believe what I believe, and I believe that for every dog I fed and petted, every cat allowed to sleep on my lap, horses curry-combed and rescued off the mountain—each and all will be a blessing to me, that my spirit will somehow be greeted with gratitude by theirs in the afterlife. I also believe that we must explain our cruelties to animals, the times we didn't care for them as we should have, our lapses in meeting our responsibilities to animals. I believe that my spirit will meet that toad's spirit and I will have to atone for and try to explain . . .

. . . why I cut off his little left hand. Because the mean older boy told me to. Because that's the only way he would let me carry his pocketknife. Because I wasn't brave enough to say No. Because he did it first, cutting off a foot, and then I did what he told me, and I cut off that little hand and the toad opened its mouth in agony but did not make a sound. In the dust of a pasture road, we buried him alive with his severed foot and hand. The older boy thought it was funny that I would cry about a goddamn toad, taking back his knife and leaving me ashamed of myself, not for crying but for what I had just done. And I have been ashamed of myself for more than half a century for that singular act of senseless, sustained cruelty.

I must never forget that sin even as I hope, in the afterlife, when I ask for forgiveness . . . I hope I am shown more generosity than I showed my dying father.

Finally, remember that in the end, all that ultimately matters is what you've done. Not what you've said, or promised, or intended. This is a hard lesson for me because I can talk a great game. I would like talk to count. But it doesn't, not in the final tally. If I've told someone I love her and have not demonstrated my love with fidelity and care and long-term commitment, then, in the end, my talk of love matters little. If I intended to live an honorable life but failed to treat people honorably, then in the end my intentions mean nothing. Too often we believe that our explanations counterbalance our actions. I didn't make it to your birthday party because I had a deadline to meet. All that counts is, I didn't make it to your birthday party. Or we try to excuse ourselves: I didn't do a good job of being a father to you because I was wrestling with my own demons. All that matters is, I didn't do a good job of being a father to you. At the end of your life, at the very summation of your life, all that matters is what you've done. The love you've shown friends. The devotion you've given your family. A house you built. Money you gave away. The dogs you raised and loved. A stamp collection you amassed. This is the thirteenth book I've published. It doesn't matter what effort it took for me to write them. It doesn't matter how far back from the pack I had to start in the race to become a writer. It doesn't matter what else was going on in my life. All that matters is that I wrote the books and they are published and people read them. I'd like to write thirteen more, but what I'd like to do doesn't count in the end. That's the latest lesson I learned—if it's important to you, do it. Because not doing it, while having a good excuse, doesn't mean anything in the end.

2 1

HOW I KEEP THE DEAD ALIVE

WHEN I was holding the revolver to my forehead and watching the hammer pull back, something other than my son's words were in that little room with me, were rooting for me not to fire the gun. I sensed, as I often do in bad times, that people I knew who've died were with me. I feel this strongly enough that I keep a list. Ever so often I take it out and go through the names, stopping at each to remember a little something about that person. It seems to me that my thinking about that person keeps him or her alive—because we don't truly die, we aren't truly gone-gone, as long as at least one person alive on earth occasionally thinks of us. Going over my list is how I keep the dead alive, how I return the favors they showed me in life.

If I'm hazy on a name, I put down a description of the person. Spellings might be fuzzy but my memories of the person are sharp. Sometimes I'll remember someone I've forgotten to put on my list and I'll add that name with my apologies. The list is not in chronological order or by rank of how important someone is to me—it's just how I remembered them. Here, I'll show you.

- **Brother Eric.** He shot himself in the head a few days before I received these pages to proof. He was funny and handsome and truly an artist. But in the end, at age forty-six, he was unable to outrun his beast.
- **Sister Linda.** Her death was a shock because she went to bed one night, had a heart attack in her sleep, and never woke up. She was in her forties, with young children. We love her and miss her. I think of her often, especially when I hear from her daughter, Kelly, and son, John.
- **My father.** The older I become, the more interesting it would've been to have the old man around.
- **Grandma Morris.** She made it clear that I was her favorite grandchild, which sometimes was embarrassing with the other grandkids but being someone's favorite is splendid. I wish that for each of you—that at some point in your life you are someone's favorite.
- **Grandpa Morris.**
- **Grandma Martin.**
- **Grandpa Martin.**
- **Rodney Cruthis.** I went to high school with him. Rodney's older brother, Chuck, and I used to torment Rodney. Sometimes, driving in the country, if we all got out to pee, Chuck and I would jump back in the car and take off, stopping 50 yards or so down the road for Rodney to run and catch up. But when he reached the car, we'd take off again. Then we'd stop, tell him the joke's over, come on, we're in a hurry now. And he'd come running up to the car and just as he was reaching the door, we'd take off again. How many times could we do that to him? How elaborate would our assurances have to become to convince him that *this* time we wouldn't pull away? He would get angry and his anger would last approximately thirty seconds after he finally got into the car. Then he'd be cracking his jokes and making his outlandish claims regarding what roughneck boy he could beat up if he wanted to and what beautiful and unattainable girl he could screw if he chose to. My dad thought Rodney was a stitch—called him Ace. Rodney survived combat in Vietnam,

survived a train hitting his UPS truck, survived cancer, and then a few years ago died of it.

- **The old woman reporter** I met when I first started writing education stories.
- **My ex-wife's grandmother,** a fascinating and ferocious old woman.
- **Hugh.** Hugh was a friend of my ex-wife's family but became my friend. He was a classic English gentleman—well read, well traveled, well bred. I don't know if he drank more alcohol than any other individual I've known, but he certainly drank it more constantly, starting with a beer and a screwdriver for breakfast. He was also a champion smoker. I was with him at a bar when he began coughing so ferociously that I thought he might end up in the hospital—a long, strangling, breath-gasping coughing spell that soon quieted the entire bar as everyone waited to see what was going to happen to this man. He finally stopped, caught his breath, and broke the awkward silence by declaring to the bar, "Won't be long now." Everyone laughed. Hugh suffered bouts of depression so debilitating that he sometimes literally could not speak. Hugh loved books and I loved talking books with him. After he died, his family discovered he had been supporting several people. Paying rents. Paying tuitions. Individuals who weren't related to him. Just people who needed help. Hugh was Catholic. The good kind. So when I get to heaven, Hugh and I can have another drink together.
- **Dillard Gibson,** the farmer who went with my father and me on a strange fishing trip to Florida. When I was eight years old, I had walked out our half-mile lane to get the mail and, walking back, I saw Mr. Gibson waving to me from a field where he had stopped his tractor. I went over, and he asked me if I liked kitty cats. I said I did. He pointed out a shallow hole in the ground where there was a little black kitty cat who had become scared of the tractor and buried itself in that hole with nothing but its tail sticking out. All I had to do was grab it by the tail and pull it out of that hole and I could take it home to my mommy. This was the first summer we were on the farm so I know I was eight years old, trusting, obedient to adults, a little kid. I went over to the hole

and saw the black tail. "Go on there, pull it out," he said, turning
to hurry to his tractor. With the mail tucked under one arm, I
grabbed that black tail with my other hand and pulled as hard as
I could. It was a skunk. Sprayed me right in the face. I remember
the foul substance hitting my upper lip and I remember that the
sensation was so horrible that I dropped the mail and ran half a
mile home to get water for my face. As the story got told later,
apparently Mr. Gibson laughed so hard he actually had to stop
his tractor and get off and fall to the ground laughing. He later
brought our mail over. Forever after that, I was Cat Boy to him.

- **Mr. Sherlock.** He was another neighbor farmer when I was
growing up. Always had a short cigar in his mouth. I never
saw him with a fresh one, just that little stub. He grew grapes
and made wine. Raised his own popcorn. I always thought
of him as a jolly old guy, an agricultural George Burns,
including even the cigar and jokes. But one time my father
and I were looking for cows that had got out and we ended up
at Mr. Sherlock's place after midnight and he didn't know
who it was and came to the door with a big-ass pistol in his
hand and a look on his face that said somebody could get shot.
An old man, rough and ready.
- **Aunt Velma.**
- **Uncle Bud.**
- **Aunt Evelyn.**
- **Uncle Jesse.**
- **Aunt Anna May.**
- **Uncle Johnny.**
- **Uncle Shorty.**
- **Uncle Bob.**
- I remember all these aunts and uncles; they were good people
and for each one I have a special memory that keeps them alive
in my mind—a joke one told, a watch one gave me, Aunt Evelyn
serving me the first tacos I'd ever eaten.
- **Jim Betchkal,** who taught me to love language and drink heavily.
- **Someone's nanny.**
- **Perry Stewart.**

• **Janet.** She was a beautiful woman, and she and I had an affair
after she'd been operated on for cancer, having had her left breast
removed. Whenever we had sex, just about every time after we
had sex, she would accuse me of having reached for her missing
breast while we were having intercourse. I would deny it. My
hand might have brushed that part of her chest but I wasn't
reaching for it. Yes you were, she would say. You forgot it was
gone and reached for it. For some reason she had to believe I was
doing that. A year after the affair ended, she came to my office
and said she'd just been told that the cancer was terminal and she
was going to die within two months. Then she sat there in that
chair across from my desk and waited for what I would say, how
I would respond. This moment was among the half-dozen most
shameful moments of my life. I'll tell you what I should've done,
I should've said, "Let's go to Vegas." Or the beach. Or New York
City. I should've taken her somewhere. Held her in my arms.
Watched a movie with her. I should have written her a poem.
Or made love to her while remembering not to reach for that
missing breast. But instead, I didn't even take her for a drink.
I asked something mealy-mouthed about whether or not she
received comfort from her faith. I know the passionate, poetic
Guys in the Back Row were screaming at me, "You wimpy
stupid shameful asshole! Close your office door and go over
there and put your arms around her! Where's your fucking soul?
If I wasn't stuck here in your head I'd leave, I'm so ashamed of
you." But this was one of the periods during my first marriage
when I was trying to be a good husband and a successful middle-
class businessman—and not a renegade artist. What a terrible
ambition. Few of the things I did while flying close to the edge
were as shameful as the way I treated Janet while I was trying to
be respectable. And nothing the Guys in the Back Row shouted
was worse than the expression on Janet's face. She didn't say
anything. She just watched me. Here I'm giving you an opportunity, her expression said, and I'm waiting to see if you're going to
do something honorable with it. When I botched my chance, she

got up and left without speaking another word, didn't even say goodbye, and she died, as promised, within two months. This is all I have left to do for her, to come across her name on my list and keep her alive for a few minutes by remembering our affair and how funny she was and smart, and recalling the precise notes of her beautiful, musical laugh.

- **Mrs. Henderson.** A grade-school teacher who really liked me.
- **Joseph Martin.**
- **Johnny Nieman.**
- **Bob Parker.** I talk slowly with pauses along the way but, compared to Bob, I am a motor mouth. I loved listening to him tell a story, taking a Jimmy Stewart stroll through the narrative, and amusing himself to no end. Bob was one of the good guys. He did not deserve the rough way he went.
- **Aunt Blanche.**
- **Uncle Harry.**
- **Man with the wooden leg.** I think he married into the family and was not a blood relative. I would see him only at family reunions and weddings, funerals. He was a happy man and I was a little boy absolutely fascinated that he had a wooden leg. He would sit me on his lap and let me thump it. One time his wife's sewing was nearby, and he pulled out a needle and told me to go ahead and stick it in his leg, it wouldn't hurt . . . wooden leg, you know. And I did and he let a terrible scream and shouted, "Wrong leg!" and I was mortified until he laughed and told me he was just kidding, and then to prove it he thumped the leg I had just stuck with the needle.
- **Mildred Bayon.**
- **Robert Bayon.**
- **Allen.** A kid I went to school with. A bully who had a beautiful voice and loved music. His mother was a sweetheart, small and timid. His father was large and terrifying. They lived in a basement house. I don't know if this happens anymore but back then sometimes a family would start building a house, get the basement dug and poured, the foundation laid, the first floor nailed

in, and then for some reason would tarpaper over the top of it and live in the basement until they got around to finishing the house. Allen killed himself several years ago.

- **Geraldine and Josh.** She struggled for several years with cancer and died of it just as I was finishing this book. Twenty-four hours before her death, her son, Josh, in his early thirties, apparently miscalculated the prescription medications he was taking and died. Larry, who was Geraldine's husband and Josh's father, is an honorable man and a hero of mine.
- **Others.** Someone who knows me will read this list and say how in God's name could I have forgotten so-and-so. I will be chagrined, but no harm done. I will add the person to my list and keep him or her in my thoughts. And if I know you and you die before me, be comforted in the certainty that I'll keep you on my list for as long as I live. To paraphrase Bill Murray in *Caddyshack*, "At least you have that going for you."

Thornton Wilder wrote that the bridge between the land of the living and the land of the dead is love. To *love* I would add *memory*.

I imagine souls in eternal serenity, some state inexplicable to us, and messages come to them periodically (although periodically and eternity are probably not compatible concepts); and the souls are told, hey, somebody living is thinking of you. Good thoughts? Yes, they're remembering when the two of you went fishing. And, hearing this, a soul smiles.

EPILOGUE AND AFTERMATH

THERE'S A real theory about how the brain works (as opposed to my theory about Guys in the Back Row and External Reality Teams) that postulates there's no there, there. Researchers have not found a specific location in the brain that is responsible for establishing a sense of ourselves. Instead, we know who we are through a narrative that is assembled from disparate parts of the mind—memory, instincts, emotions. And that assembled narrative is in fact our consciousness, our sense of who we are. It is our story. This story gets edited, added to, changed over the years, but continually telling the story of ourselves is how we know we exist.

I'm working on my story. I'm tweaking the main character to make him less arrogant, less of a know-it-all. It's strange that as I get older and acquire additional knowledge, I become all the more vividly aware of my ignorance.

I'll give you an example. I've always believed that character is destiny, that if you know someone's true character, you can pretty much map out how your association with that person will unfold. If the person's character is honorable, you will be treated honorably. If the person's character is selfish, then you will have to give more to the person than you'll ever receive.

Whenever I told someone that character is destiny, I would cite Aesop's fable:

A scorpion asked a frog for a ride across the pond. The frog, already in the water and therefore safe from the non-swimming scorpion, declined. "If I give you a ride, you'll sting me." But the scorpion said, "Think about it. I can't swim. If we're crossing the pond and I sting you, you'll die and sink and I'll then drown. Why would I do that?" This made sense to the frog, so he agreed. The scorpion crawled on the frog's back and off they went. Halfway across the pond, the scorpion stings the frog. As the frog is about to die, he manages to ask, "Why did you do that? Now we'll both die." The scorpion replied sadly, "I could do no other—it is my character."

But it's not always true. Sometimes you can carry that scorpion across the water without getting stung. I recently worked with someone whose character changed dramatically—from an awful person who was overbearing and mean-spirited to a delightful, supportive friend. What happened? I don't know. But this particular change in character is just one of many examples of how wrong I've been in my life.

I'm glad that character isn't destiny and that destiny isn't immutable, because my character, my tendency toward tragedy and drama, has always led me toward a certain bleakness:

I am eating Campbell's turkey noodle soup with a fork, directly from the can, the soup salted only with my tears as I sit on a folding chair at a bare table overhung with a 40-watt incandescent bulb partially shielded by a paper shade, torn in places and scorched in others. The house has a yard of bare dirt on a street with no name.

It hasn't turned out that way. Instead I've bought a house in the country with my sister and I've planted a garden and each day now I bring in corn and tomatoes. It is surprisingly healthy. And instead of quitting my job, I'm working half-time, using the other half to write. These reasonable choices seem out of character for me. Like I said, I'm working on the story.

Still, I'm a novelist, an artist, and I've told my farm-boy Guy in the Back Row to stop being embarrassed by that assertion. I have books to write. For a while, I lost my way as a writer and tried to chase sales and write to a formula, but now I've become serious again about writing. I want to live a writer's life. I want the story of me to include chapters of living in Europe. I want the story to include scenes where I wake up a woman sleeping next to me and take her outside to see a blood-red moonrise.

People I have talked with who have lost everything did not report finding happiness. In fact, some of them said they had never even stopped hurting. But what many told me, and what I discovered for myself, is that if you're lucky and if you keep pushing and pulling those carts, then what you carry through life eventually becomes *bearable*.

Take heart. Or as Wisdom on the Mountain once told me, "When life withers hope, call on courage." And for chrissakes, don't kill yourself. Because if you're lucky like me, you'll find that the more you're lost, the closer to home you'll be.

ACKNOWLEDGMENTS

Not to brag, but here's an accounting of the wealth I've managed to accumulate over the years.

Long-term investments:
Nancy Martin
Matthew Martin
Joshua Martin
Marilyn Cutler
Barbara Parker
Johanna Crighton
Ambrose Clancy
Mary Lydon
David Rosenthal
Bob Neff
Kathy Martin

Mid-term investments:
Jon Carlock
Myra Carlock
Joe Hartley
Amanda Martin

New investments:
Pearl Lucille Martin
Samuel Lucius Martin
Beverly Barnes
Kerri Kolen
Jay Winer Nightwolf

ABOUT THE AUTHOR

DAVID LOZELL MARTIN'S previous novels include interna-
tional bestsellers *Lie to Me* and *Tap, Tap,* and the critically acclaimed
The Crying Heart Tattoo, The Beginning of Sorrows, and *Crazy Love. Losing
Everything* is his first work of nonfiction. He lives in the Washington,
D.C., area.